SECOND EDITION

Culinary Calculations

Simplified Math for Culinary Professionals

TERRI JONES

BICENTENNIAL
1807
WILEY
2007
BICENTENNIAL

JOHN WILEY & SONS, INC.

Published by John Wiley & Sons, Inc., Hoboken, New Jersey
Published simultaneously in Canada

Wiley Bicentennial Logo: Richard J. Pacifico

For general information on our other products and services, or technical support, please contact our Customer Care Department within the United States at 800-762-2974, outside the United States at 317-572-3993 or fax 317-572-4002.

Wiley also publishes its books in a variety of electronic formats. Some content that appears in print may not be available in electronic books.

For more information about Wiley products, visit our Web site at http://www.wiley.com.

Library of Congress Cataloging-in-Publication Data:

Jones, Terri, 1954–
    Culinary calculations : simplified math for culinary professionals / by Terri Jones. — 2nd ed.
        p. cm.
    Includes index.
    ISBN: 978-0-471-74816-8 (pbk. : alk. paper)
    1. Food service—Mathematics.   I. Title.
    TX911.3.M33J56 2007
    647.9501′51—dc22

Printed in the United States of America

10 9 8 7 6 5 4 3 2 1

Contents

SECTION I: Basic Mathematics for the Foodservice Industry   5

CHAPTER 5: BASIC MATHEMATICS: ADDITIONAL INFORMATION AND TIPS FOR SUCCESS   50

SECTION II: Mathematics for the Professional Kitchen   **61**

SECTION III: Mathematics for the Business side of the Foodservice Industry   135

CHAPTER 11: MENU PRICING   137

CHAPTER 12: BASIC ACCOUNTING FOR FOODSERVICE OPERATIONS: ALSO KNOWN AS THE IMPACT OF MENU PRICING ON SUCCESS AND PROFIT   153

SECTION IV: Computer Applications for the Foodservice Industry 187

Preface

The second edition of *Culinary Calculations* focuses on understanding the importance of mathematics to a successful career in the foodservice industry. This edition contains several new features and is divided into four distinct sections. Each chapter begins with a list of learning objectives to help you focus in on the key material. Boxed formula frames are used throughout the text to highlight all of the formulas. All multistep processes, such as costing a recipe, are also enclosed in a formula frame. Quick tips have been inserted throughout the text to further clarify and explain difficult concepts.

The feature that engages the audience and sets this text apart from the rest is the addition of a running case study. The purpose of this case study is to integrate the foodservice mathematics you are learning with the hypothetical scenario of opening a profitable, and therefore successful, foodservice operation. This newly added running case study actively involves you in the planning phase of opening a hypothetical restaurant as you work through the chapters of the text.

Section I, "Basic Mathematics for the Foodservice Industry," contains five chapters. Each chapter in this section explains basic mathematical concepts necessary to master for success in the foodservice industry. Chapter 1 explains addition, subtraction, multiplication, and division with whole numbers. Chapter 2 explains the process for solving applied math problems for real-life situations. Chapter 3 is an introduction to mixed numbers and noninteger quantities, commonly referred to as fractions, decimals, and percents. Chapter 4 explains addition, subtraction, multiplication, and division with mixed numbers and noninteger quantities. Chapter 5 explains additional mathematical concepts and terminology helpful to students in the foodservice industry including ratios and proportions.

Section II, "Mathematics for the Professional Kitchen," contains five chapters. Each chapter in this section explains how the foodservice industry purchases and prepares food products to create a successful restaurant. Chapter 6 explains standardized recipes and recipe yield quantities. Step I of the running case study is the selection of menu items, which sets the tone for a new restaurant. The corresponding menu items' recipes are then placed onto standardized recipe forms. Then for Step II of the running case study, the recipes' yields are adjusted to serve 50 guests. Chapter 7 explains the differing units of measure used in a professional kitchen. Step III of the running case study involves adjusting and correcting the units of measure on the standardized recipe forms. Chapter 8 explains the foodservice-specific terminology used in the professional kitchen. Chapter 9 explains the impact of as-purchased and edible portions on the major food groups. Chapter 10 explains recipe and portion costing. Step IV of the running case study costs out the recipes and portion sizes you have selected.

Section III, "Mathematics for the Business Side of the Foodservice Industry," contains four chapters. Each chapter explains in detail the concepts of running a profitable restaurant. Chapter 11 explains the many facets of menu pricing. Step V of the running case study involves pricing the menus you have developed. Chapter 12 explains basic accounting and the impact of menu pricing on a restaurant's success. Step VI of the running case study encourages you to create a projected profit and loss statement and to critique the menu prices developed in Step V. Chapter 13 explains the high cost of labor in the foodservice industry and provides techniques to control labor costs. Step VII of the running case study involves developing mock schedules for the job categories in your hypothetical restaurant to help you understand labor cost control. Chapter 14 explains inventory management and its impact on profitability. Step VIII of the running case study involves comparing the food cost on the profit and loss statement to determine if the quantity of products in inventory is correct.

Section IV, "Computer Applications for the Foodservice Industry" contains one chapter. Chapter 15 explains the variety of computer software applications used in the foodservice industry today. Step IX is the final step in the running case study. You are asked to determine the types of computer applications you will use in your hypothetical restaurant.

The *Second Edition* of *Culinary Calculations* was written to further your knowledge and to sharpen your business skills so you can enjoy a successful career in the foodservice industry. I hope you enjoy learning from the edition as much as I have enjoyed sharing my knowledge with you.

Terri Jones

Additional Resources

An *Instructor's Manual* (ISBN 978-0-470-04508-4) includes the following for each chapter:

- The introduction provides a brief overview of the chapter.
- The learning objectives allow you to focus your students on the key points in each chapter.
- Vocabulary is provided and defined to help identify the key concepts in each chapter.
- Chapter outlines show the overall structure of the chapters.
- Test/quiz questions, including true/false, multiple choice, and some problems, provide materials different from the exercises in the book and can serve as a test bank.

A companion Web site includes electronic files for the *Instructor's Manual with Test Questions.*

Acknowledgments

I would like to thank the following instructors for their insightful feedback during the course of the development of my revised material for the *Second Edition:*

Marcia Hajduk, Harrisburg Area Community College
Kimberly Johnson, Syracuse University
Virginia Stipp Lawrence, Austin Community College
Bill Lembke, Orlando Culinary Academy
Clifford Wener, College of Lake County
Eric Wynkoop, Western Culinary Institute

Introduction *to* Culinary Calculations

The Importance of Mathematics to a Successful Career in the Foodservice Industry

". . . the courses culinary students struggle with the most tend to be accounting and math . . . "

This quote, from *Chef Educator Today*, Autumn 2005, highlights the need for foodservice students to develop a solid foundation in basic mathematics. This foundation will enhance their understanding of the mathematical applications used in the kitchen and the business side of the industry. The foodservice industry has many unique mathematical characteristics, all of them based on basic mathematics.

 ## Mathematics in the Kitchen

Food is often purchased in a unit of measure that is different than the unit of measure used in a recipe, or the unit of measure used to serve the guest. Mathematics is the key to unit of measure conversions. Most foods shrink during preparation. This impacts the actual quantity of food that should be prepared for service. Mathematics is the key to proper preparation quantities. In addition, many food products are perishable. Perishability, or shelf life, can impact the quantity of product needed to serve guests. Mathematics is the key to determining the optimal amount of food to keep in storage.

Properly prepared recipes will produce a specific number of portions only if the portions are sized correctly. Mathematics ensures that recipes produce the stated number of portions and the portions are sized correctly.

These examples prove mathematics is essential for a successful career in the professional kitchen.

Mathematics for Foodservice Operations

All commercial foodservice operations, and many noncommercial, or on-site operations, are for-profit businesses. This means the business must generate enough sales revenue to cover all of the costs of doing business and have money left over. This leftover money is the profit. Even nonprofit foodservice operations must adhere to a strict budget, or management might be terminated. Mathematics is used to track sales revenue, the costs of doing business, budgets, and, hopefully, the profit.

Mathematics is also used to determine the cost of the food served to a guest and is critical for developing menu prices. Remember, the menu prices provide the sales revenue. Certain mathematical calculations ensure the foodservice operation has a viable profit structure so it can be a successful business.

Case Study: Applied Mathematics in the Foodservice Industry

Case studies are valuable tools used to introduce different concepts related to a specific industry or business. Case studies are used in this text to highlight important mathematical issues in the foodservice industry. Beginning in Section II of this book, a running case study is integrated within each chapter to help illustrate the mathematical applications in the foodservice industry.

Following is one example of a case study that introduces the importance of effective mathematical decision making in the foodservice industry. This example illustrates that one mathematical mistake can have significant consequences for a business. Hopefully, this case study will reinforce the need for you to develop a strong background in foodservice mathematics.

This is the true story of a costly mathematical mistake made by a major U.S. seafood restaurant chain. The chain was searching for a new promotion to increase customer counts chain-wide. A company vice president came up with the idea of an all-you-can-eat crab leg special. This vice president mathematically estimated that the average customer would eat two portions of crab legs.

The all-you-can-eat crab leg special was advertised nationwide. It was available for one month. At the end of the month, the company realized the average customer ate three portions of crab legs, not two, as the vice president had originally estimated. The actual cost to serve each guest was one portion of crab legs greater than the original estimate. This became a very expensive mathematical mistake.

Customer counts did increase, but the cost of the all-you-can-eat crab leg special was underestimated. The actual food cost for each guest who bought the special was $\frac{1}{3}$ (.33, or 33%) higher than projected. As a result, the company's quarterly profit declined by 12% and the vice president resigned.

This case study is a true-life example of how easy it is to make a costly mathematical mistake in the foodservice industry. Should this vice president have spent more time in the planning phase of this promotion? Would better planning have helped to avoid the financial disaster that unfolded? Are there any lessons to be learned from this case study?

The vice president should have pretested the special at one or more units of the chain to determine the actual number of portions of crab legs the average guest would eat before the special was introduced chain-wide. He also should have completed several what-if scenarios, along with financial projections, to determine if the menu price of the special was high enough to provide adequate sales revenue. For instance, "what if the average guest eats more than two portions" should have been considered before the promotion was rolled out nationally.

There are many mathematical scenarios that should have been explored to ensure the promotion would be successful both in increasing customer counts and profit for the chain. This case study proves that mathematics is a valuable tool to use for making sound business decisions.

Conclusion

The importance of a solid foundation in basic mathematics to a successful career in the foodservice industry cannot be overstated. Mathematics is associated with most of the daily activities that take place in the professional kitchen and in foodservice operations. The proper use of mathematics helps to ensure the profitability of a foodservice operation.

BASIC
MATHEMATICS
for the
FOODSERVICE
INDUSTRY

CHAPTER 1

Basic Mathematics *with* Whole Numbers

"The foundation is built before the house is constructed."

—TERRI JONES

Having basic mathematical knowledge is critical to a successful career in the culinary and foodservice industry. Basic mathematics includes addition, subtraction, multiplication, and division with whole numbers. This chapter reviews these concepts.

LEARNING OBJECTIVES

1. To review basic mathematical operations and their properties
2. To review addition, subtraction, multiplication, and division using whole numbers in typical foodservice situations

Whole Numbers

The system used, the Hindu–Arabic numeration system, is a decimal place-value system. This system is based on the number 10 and uses symbols called **digits** or **integers**. The digits or integers are 0, 1, 2, 3, 4, 5, 6, 7, 8, and 9. Whole numbers may consist of one or more digits.

Place Value

Each place a digit occupies in a number has a value called a **place value**. Each place value increases from right to left, and each increase is 10 times the value of the place to the right. The place values are arranged in **periods**, or groups of three. The first period is called **ones**, the second is called **thousands**, the third is called **millions**, and so on. Within each period is a **ones** place, a **tens** place, and a **hundreds** place. Commas are used to set off groups of three-digit numbers.

1	One
100	One Hundred
1,000	One Thousand
1,000,000	One Million
1,000,000,000	One Billion

 Numbers Written as Words

Numbers can be written as words. We work from left to right, writing the numbers in each group, followed by the group name. Additional rules apply to this method:

1. The name of the *ones* group is not written.
2. The word *and* is not used.
3. The numbers from 21 to 99, except 30, 40, 50, and so forth, use a hyphen when they are written.
4. A period containing all zeros is skipped.

> The number 2,342 is written as:
> Two thousand, three hundred, forty-two.

 Addition

Addition is the combining of two or more groups of the same kind to arrive at a **sum.** The symbol for addition is the "plus" sign, or "+." Addition has three properties:

1. *Commutative property.* Numbers can be added in any order:

   $1 + 2 = 3$ or $2 + 1 = 3$

2. *Associative property.* Numbers can be grouped in any order:

   $(4 + 5) + 6 = 15$ or $4 + (5 + 6) = 15$

3. *Zero identity property.* Adding zero to any number results in the same number:

   $7 + 0 = 7$ or $0 + 7 = 7$

ADDITION EXAMPLE

Addition is used to total a guest check. Three guests place an order from an à la carte menu. The guest-check items are added to arrive at a sum or the total amount of money the guests owe for their meals.

À LA CARTE MENU

ITEM A $3
ITEM B $4
ITEM C $5
ITEM D $6
ITEM E $7

Items B, D, and E are ordered. The food server adds the guest check:

Item B + Item D + Item E = Guest-check sum

$$\$4 + \$6 + \$7 = \$17, \quad \text{or} \quad \begin{array}{r} \$4 \\ \$6 \\ + \$7 \\ \hline \$17 \end{array}$$

The guest-check sum is $17.

Addition is used daily in foodservice operations to add guest counts, guest checks, purchase quantities, labor costs, recipe costs, and sales revenue.

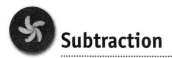

Subtraction

Subtraction is the deducting, or taking away, of one number from another to arrive at the **difference**. The symbol for subtraction is the "minus" sign, or "–."Subtraction is the opposite of addition. It does *not* have the following properties:

1. *Commutative property.* Subtraction is not commutative:

   $2 - 1 = 1$, but $1 - 2$ does not equal 1.

2. *Associative property.* Subtraction is not associative:

   $5 - (4 - 3) = 4$, but $(5 - 4) - 3$ does not equal 4.

3. *Zero identity property.* Subtraction does not have zero identity.

6 − 0 = 6, but 0 − 6 does not equal 6.

SUBTRACTION EXAMPLE

Item E was not to the guest's liking. The food server subtracts the cost of Item E from the guest check.

> Guest-check sum − Item E = Revised guest-check sum
>
> $17 − $7 = $10,   or $17
>
>   − $7
>   ─────────
> $10
>
> The revised guest-check sum is $10.

Subtraction is also used daily in foodservice operations. Daily inventory usage is subtracted from beginning inventory levels to determine purchase requirements. Subtraction is used to take away costs from sales, to determine profit for individual menu items, and to calculate gross profit and total profit or loss for a foodservice operation.

Multiplication

Multiplication is the adding of a number to itself a certain number of times to arrive at a **product.** It abbreviates the process of repeated addition. The symbol for multiplication is the "times" sign, or "×." Multiplication has the following properties:

1. *Commutative property.* Numbers can be multiplied in any order:

   $1 \times 2 = 2$ or $2 \times 1 = 2$

2. *Associative property.* Numbers can be grouped in any manner:

   $(3 \times 4) \times 5 = 60$ or $3 \times (4 \times 5) = 60$

3. *Zero property.* The product of a number and zero is zero:

   $7 \times 0 = 0$ or $0 \times 7 = 0$

4. *Multiplicative identity property.* Multiplying any number by 1 results in the same number:

   $8 \times 1 = 8$ or $1 \times 8 = 8$

5. *Distributive property.* Multiplying a sum or a difference by a factor is equivalent to multiplying each term of the sum or difference by the factor:

   $2 \times (3 + 4) = 2 \times 7 = 14$ or $2 \times (3 + 4) = (2 \times 3) + (2 \times 4) = 6 + 8 = 14$

   $4 \times (3 − 2) = 4 \times 1 = 4$ or $4 \times (3 − 2) = (4 \times 3) − (4 \times 2) = 12 − 8 = 4$

QUICK TIP: Appendix I contains a Math Facts Multiplication Grid. Use it to review your multiplication facts.

MULTIPLICATION EXAMPLE

TJ's Hotel offers three banquet menus. A guest would like the total cost of each menu to serve 50 people. Multiplying the cost per menu times the number of guests will determine the total cost for each banquet menu.

BANQUET MENU CHOICES

MENU I:	**$32**
MENU II:	**$42**
MENU III:	**$52**

Menu I: 50 × $32 = $1,600,   or

$$\begin{array}{r} \$32 \\ \times\, 50 \\ \hline \$1{,}600 \end{array}$$

Menu II: 50 × $42 = $2,100,   or

$$\begin{array}{r} \$42 \\ \times\, 50 \\ \hline \$2{,}100 \end{array}$$

Menu III: 50 × $52 = $2,600,   or

$$\begin{array}{r} \$52 \\ \times\, 50 \\ \hline \$2{,}600 \end{array}$$

The total cost to serve 50 guests: Menu I $1,600.00, Menu II $2,100.00, and Menu III $2,600.00

Multiplication is used daily in foodservice operations to determine the total price of multiple quantities of items on a purchase order, the total cost of more than one of the same menu items, or anytime repeated addition will yield the correct answer.

Division

Division is the process of determining how many times one number is contained within another number. It is the opposite of multiplication. The **divisor (b)** is divided into the **dividend (a)**. The answer is called the **quotient.** There are four symbols to represent division:

$$a\big/b \qquad \frac{a}{b} \qquad b\overline{)a} \qquad a \div b \cdot$$

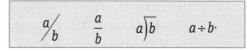

Division does *not* have the following:

1. *Commutative property.* Division is not commutative:

   $12 \div 6 = 2$, but $6 \div 12$ does not equal 2

2. *Associative property.* Division is not associative.

   $(12 \div 6) \div 2 = 2 \div 2 = 1$, but $12 \div (6 \div 2) = 12 \div 3 = 4$

3. *Zero division rules:*

   a. Zero divided by a nonzero number equals 0:

      $0 \div 3 = 0$

   b. Any number divided by zero is undefined:

      $3 \div 0 =$ Undefined

   c. Zero divided by zero is indeterminate:

      $0 \div 0 =$ Indeterminate

4. *Divisibility identity property.* Any number divided by 1 results in the same number:

   $4 \div 1 = 4$

DIVISION EXAMPLE

The guest interested in holding the banquet for 50 people would like to spend a total of $2,000. What would the menu price be if 50 (divisor) guests were served for $2,000 (dividend)? The cost per person, or menu price, is determined by dividing 50 people into the $2,000. The menu price is $40.00.

$$\$2,000 \Big/ {}_{50} = \$40$$

$$\frac{\$2,000}{50} = \$40$$

$$50\overline{)2,000}\ \ \overset{40}{}$$

$$\$2,000 \div 50 = \$40$$

Division is used daily in foodservice operations to determine the cost per portion from the total cost of a recipe, the average cost per guest, the average guest check, and inventory turnover rate.

 ## Conclusion

The basic mathematical operations of addition, subtraction, multiplication, and division are used daily in the professional kitchen and foodservice business office. A solid understanding of these operations is critical for a successful career in the foodservice industry.

Basic Mathematics with Whole Numbers:
REVIEW PROBLEMS

Addition

1. 32 + 56 =

2. 267 + 389 =

3. 539 + 884 =

4. 1,117 + 206 =

5. 2,064 + 1,896 =

6. 1,245
 + 2,456

7. 2,654
 + 800

8. 10,538
 + 12,662

9. 124,368
 + 189,960

10. 1,650,324
 + 2,895,421

Subtraction

1. 67 − 23 =

2. 54 − 33 =

3. 123 − 98 =

4. 1,064 − 889 =

5. 2,657 − 1, 559 =

6.   654
 − 550

7. 1,112
 − 678

8. 15,693
 − 9,872

9. 259,654
 − 112,399

10. 5,678,321
 − 2,889,450

Multiplication

1. 10 × 2 =

2. 45 × 4 =

3. 105 × 6 =

4. 1,234 × 5 =

5. 2,500 × 8 =

6. 65
　　× 5
　　─────

7. 80
　　× 7
　　─────

8. 250
　　× 4
　　─────

9. 300
　　× 40
　　─────

10. 2,500
　　× 60
　　─────

Division

1. 20/5 =

2. 60 ÷ 12 =

3. 10)‾9‾0‾0‾

4. $\dfrac{90}{45}$ =

5. 250/5 =

6. 1,200 ÷ 300 =

7. 22)‾2‾2‾,‾0‾0‾0‾

8. $\dfrac{2,004}{12}$ =

9. 10,000/250 =

10. 25,000 ÷ 25 =

11. 15)‾6‾0‾0‾

12. $\dfrac{800}{40}$ =

CHAPTER **2**

Applied Math Problems
with Simple Solutions

"Math principles are much more important to students than just learning to follow recipes or formulas in cooking or baking—it teaches them to be good problem solvers."

—Joseph "Mick" La Lopa, Ph.D., instructor and writer, *Chef Educator*

In the professional kitchen or foodservice business office, a mathematical problem will not always present itself in the format of an equation. It can be associated with a complicated real-life situation or problem, and often requires immediate attention. How do you determine which mathematical solution will solve the problem? This chapter answers this question.

LEARNING OBJECTIVES

1. To understand the process for solving an applied math problem
2. To determine which mathematical operation to use when solving an applied math problem
3. To use the four-step method to assist you in solving an applied math problem

Solving Applied Math Problems

A simple solution for solving an applied math problem is to break the problem down into smaller pieces. Most situations or problems are multifaceted, which means there are several steps to the solution. If each facet is addressed separately, it is easier to arrive at a solution. After all of the pieces are addressed, the entire problem can be solved. The four-step method and the case study that follow illustrate how the problem can be broken down into smaller pieces, making it easier to solve any real-life mathematical-related situation or problem.

THE FOUR-STEP METHOD FOR SOLVING APPLIED MATH PROBLEMS

The **four-step method** guides you through the process for solving applied math problems. There are four steps, or questions, to consider when solving an applied math problem:

> **STEP 1:** What is the issue?
>
> **STEP 2:** What information is given?
>
> **STEP 3:** Which mathematical operation is used?
>
> **STEP 4:** Does the answer make sense?

APPLIED WORD PROBLEMS: SIMPLE SOLUTIONS

Case Study I

Chef TJ will be serving a breakfast banquet for 100 guests. Each guest will be served a three-egg omelet.

STEP 1: What is Chef TJ's issue?

Chef TJ is serving 100 three-egg omelets and needs to determine the total number of eggs to serve this banquet. Eggs are ordered by the dozen. Chef TJ also needs to determine the total number of dozen eggs to order.

STEP 2: What information is given?

The information given is 100 three-egg omelets will be served. There are 12 eggs per dozen.

STEP 3: Which mathematical operation is used to find a total?

Both addition and multiplication can be used to find a total. Chef TJ could add the number 3 (eggs) to itself 100 (guests) times, or he could multiply the number 3 (eggs) by 100 (guests). The answer is the same, but multiplication is quicker and easier.

> $3 + 3 + 3 + 3 + 3 \ldots$ (100 times) $= 300$
> $3 \times 100 = 300$

Chef TJ needs 300 eggs to serve each of the 100 guests a three-egg omelet.

STEP 4:   Does the answer make sense?

Can this answer be justified? Yes, it takes 300 eggs to prepare 100 omelets each with 3 eggs. However, this problem is not complete because the eggs need to be ordered. The four-step method can be repeated to address this facet of the situation.

STEP 1:   What is Chef TJ's issue?

The issue is how many dozen eggs Chef TJ should order.

STEP 2:   What information is given?

There are 12 eggs per dozen. Chef TJ needs 300 eggs.

STEP 3:   Which mathematical operation can determine the correct number of dozen eggs to order?

Division is used to divide one number by another. Which number is the divisor and which is the dividend? Does the chef divide 300 by 12, or 12 by 300?

$$^{300}/_{12} = 25 \qquad \frac{300}{12} = 25 \qquad 12\overline{)300} = 25 \qquad 300 \div 12 = 25$$

or

$$^{12}/_{300} = 0.040 \qquad \frac{12}{300} = 0.040 \qquad 300\overline{)12} = 0.040 \qquad 12 \div 300 = 0.040$$

STEP 4:   Does the answer make sense?

Which answer can be justified? Should Chef TJ order 25 dozen eggs, or 0.040 dozen eggs? Chef TJ should order 25 dozen eggs to serve 100 guests a three-egg omelet. Therefore, the number 300 is the **dividend**, and the number 12 is the **divisor**. By dividing 300 by 12, Chef TJ knows to order 25 dozen eggs to cook 100 guests a three-egg omelet.

 *QUICK TIP:*   If an answer does not make sense, use the opposite mathematical operation. For example, if you added, try subtraction, and if you multiplied, try division. As the above example points out, perhaps the dividend and the divisor need to be reversed.

Conclusion

In the real world of the professional kitchen or the foodservice business office, a simple mathematical solution can often be found for a situation or a problem. The key to solving the situation or problem is to break it down into manageable pieces. The **four-step method** for solving applied math problems assists you in the process of breaking a problem down into more manageable and easy-to-solve pieces.

Applied Math Problems with Simple Solutions: REVIEW PROBLEMS

CASE STUDY II

A wedding for 400 guests will be served on Saturday night. The bride has 5 requests for setting the tables. Each request is a separate mathematical "issue" that should be addressed. The requests are as follows:

1. Ten guests per table.
2. Two tablecloths per table: one long white cloth and one blue overlay cloth.
3. Alternating white and blue napkins; every other guest has a different-color napkin.
4. Each guest has 2 knives, 3 forks, and 4 spoons.
5. Each guest has a water goblet, a champagne glass, and a coffee cup and saucer.

These issues are simple and can be solved without the formal process of the four-step method. However, I encourage you to use the four-step method to learn the process because the applied math problems and real-life situations that you encounter will become more difficult as you progress through the text and, eventually, your careers. I have provided information on the following pages to assist you with solving these applied math problems. After you solve each aspect of the bride's requests, you should answer the questions that follow.

REQUEST 1: Ten guests per table

STEP 1:   What is the issue?

The total number of tables needed for the wedding guests.

STEP 2:   What information is given?

There are 400 guests. Each table will have 10 guests.

STEP 3:   Which mathematical operation is used?

Division is used to determine the number of tables to serve 400 guests.

The divisor is _____. The dividend is _____.

The answer is _____.

STEP 4: Does the answer make sense?

You have divided the divisor into the dividend. Justify your answer.

REQUEST 2: Two tablecloths per table—One long white cloth and one blue overlay cloth

STEP 1: What is the issue?

The total number of long white and short blue tablecloths needed to set the tables and the total number of cloths to order.

STEP 2: What information is given?

The total number of tables was answered in Request 1.

Each table will have 2 tablecloths.

STEP 3: Which mathematical operation is used?

Addition or multiplication can be used.

STEP 4: Does the answer make sense?

Justify your answer.

REQUEST 3: Alternating white and blue napkins (every other guest has a different color)

STEP 1: What is the issue?

The total number of white and blue napkins that are needed to set the tables. Napkins are delivered in packages of 25 each. How many packages of napkins should be ordered?

STEP 2: What information is given?

The total number of tables and the number of guests per table are given.

STEP 3: Which mathematical operation is used?

Division can be used to divide the total number of guests by 2, the number of napkin choices; or multiplication can be used to multiply the number of guests at each table who will use each color of napkin by the total number of tables. Use both operations to see if the answers are indeed the same.

Next, division is used to determine the number of packages of each color of napkins to order. Which number is the divisor and which is the dividend?

STEP 4:   Does the answer make sense?

Justify your answer.

REQUEST 4: Each cover has 2 knives, 3 forks, and 4 spoons

STEP 1:   What is the issue?

The total number of knives, forks, and spoons that are needed to set the tables. Silverware is wrapped 50 pieces per package. How many packages of each type of silverware are needed to set the tables?

STEP 2:   What information is given?

The total number of guests is 400.

STEP 3:   Which mathematical operation is used?

Multiplication is used to determine the total number of each piece of silverware needed. Division is used to determine the number of packages of silverware to use.

STEP 4:   Does the answer make sense?

Justify your answer.

REQUEST 5: A water goblet, a champagne glass, and a coffee cup and saucer at each cover

STEP 1:   What is the issue?

Glasses and cups are washed and stored in plastic racks. The racks vary in size to properly hold each type of glass. There are 25 water goblets, 30 champagne glasses, and 20 coffee cups per rack. (How many racks of water goblets, champagne glasses, and coffee cups are needed to serve 400 guests?)

STEP 2:   What information is given?

Please fill this in.

STEP 3:   Which mathematical operation is used?

This issue is similar to other requests.

STEP 4: Does the answer make sense?

Justify your answer.

Now that you've completed the four-step method for each of the 5 requests, you are able to answer the following questions:

1. How many tables are needed to serve the 400 guests? _____

2. How many long white tablecloths are needed? _____

3. How many short blue overlay cloths are needed? _____

4. What is the total number of tablecloths that need to be ordered? _____

5. How many white napkins are needed? _____

6. How many blue napkins are needed? _____

7. How many bundles of napkins should be ordered? _____

8. What is the total number of knives, forks, and spoons needed to set the tables? _____

9. How many bundles of knives, forks, and spoons are needed to set the tables? _____

10. How many racks of water goblets, champagne glasses, and coffee cups are needed to set the tables? _____

CHAPTER 3

Mixed Numbers *and* Noninteger Quantities

"Most college students cannot handle many complex but common tasks, from understanding credit card offers to comparing the cost of food per ounce."

—Ben Feller, writer, *Associated Press*

A *mixed number* is a number that contains a whole number and a fractional part. A fraction, decimal, or percent is considered a noninteger quantity. A noninteger quantity is a piece, part, or portion of a whole.

Noninteger quantities are used daily in foodservice operations. Foodservice examples of a noninteger quantity incude one slice of a whole pie, one bowl from a pot of soup, or one serving from a pan of lasagna. Mathematical relationships exist between the different types of noninteger quantities.

LEARNING OBJECTIVES

1. To understand the value of a noninteger quantity
2. To understand the basic format of a fraction, decimal, and percent
3. To understand the components of a mixed number
4. To convert a fraction to a decimal and a percent
5. To convert a decimal to a percent and a fraction
6. To convert a percent to a decimal and a fraction

Fractions, Decimals, and Percents

FRACTIONS

When a unit of a whole quantity is divided into parts, we call those parts fractions of the unit. The bottom number, the **denominator**, indicates the number of parts one whole unit has been divided into. The top number, the **numerator**, is the number of parts being considered.

$$\frac{\text{Numerator}}{\text{Denominator}}$$

If the numerator is less than the denominator, the fraction represents a number less than 1 and is called a **proper fraction**. The following are examples of proper fractions:

$$\frac{1}{10} \quad \frac{1}{2} \quad \frac{3}{4}$$

If the numerator is equal to the denominator, the fraction equals 1. If the numerator is greater than the denominator, it represents a number greater than 1. Fractions that are equal to or are greater than 1 are called **improper fractions**. The following are improper fractions:

$$\frac{3}{3} \quad \frac{4}{3}$$

An improper fraction should be reduced to 1, or to a mixed number by dividing the denominator into the numerator. The numerator is the dividend and the denominator is the divisor.

$$\frac{3}{3} = \text{ or } \frac{4}{3} = 1\frac{1}{3}$$

 **QUICK TIP:** When you are using a calculator, dividing the denominator into the numerator produces the answer in decimal format, for example, $\frac{4}{3} = 1.33$. The decimal must be converted into a fraction, for example, 1.33 = 1 and 1/3. Long division produces the *quotient* with a remainder. The remainder is the numerator of the

fraction. You may find it easier to subtract the denominator from the numerator, $4 - 3 = 1$, yielding the numerator of the mixed-number fraction $\frac{4}{3} = 1\frac{1}{3}$. Remember to insert the whole number before the fraction.

Extra care is required when subtracting to ensure the correct whole number for the mixed-number fraction is used. For example, the improper fraction $\frac{33}{16}$ when reduced to a mixed-number fraction is $2\frac{1}{16}$, because 16 can be subtracted 2 times from 33 with a remainder of 1.

DECIMALS

The decimal system expresses quantities in tens, multiples of ten, tenths, hundredths, and other submultiples of 10.

Hundred	100
Ten	10
One	1
One-tenth	0.1
One-hundredth	0.01
One-thousandth	0.001

Decimals are noninteger quantities expressed by using a decimal point. The following decimal number is equal to $\frac{1}{10}$ as a decimal fraction, because the *one* decimal place represents tenths.

0.1

PERCENTS

Percentages are noninteger quantities expressed using a percent sign (%). The **"cent"** in percent means 100, so "percent" means "per 100." The percent number that follows represents $\frac{1}{10}$ as a fraction, 0.1 as a decimal, and 10% as a percent:

10%

 # Common Examples of Noninteger Quantities

The United States monetary system is a decimal-based system. Therefore, a great example of noninteter quantities is coin money: half-dollars, quarters, dimes, nickels, and pennies. Coins represent fractions, decimals, and percents of one dollar. Table 3.1 displays this concept.

TABLE 3.1 United States Coin Money Expressed as a Fraction, Decimal, and Percent of $1.00

Unit	Decimal	Fraction	Percent
One dollar	$1.00	1/1	100%
Half-dollar	$0.50	½	50%
Quarter	$0.25	¼	25%
Dime	$0.10	1/10	10%
Nickel	$0.05	1/20	5%
Penny	$0.01	1/100	1%

One dollar is the equivalent of 1/1, or 100% of itself. One half-dollar is the equivalent of ½, or 50% of one dollar. One quarter is ¼, or 25% of one dollar. One dime is $\frac{1}{10}$, or 10% of one dollar. One nickel is $\frac{1}{20}$, or 5% of one dollar. One penny is $\frac{1}{100}$, or 1% of one dollar.

FIGURE 3.1

U.S. Money

Photography by Thomas Myers

Another common example is the slicing of a whole pizza into noninteger quantities as shown in Table 3.2.

TABLE 3.2 Slices of a Pizza Expressed as a Fraction, Decimal, and Percent of a Whole Pie

Pizza	Fraction	Decimal	Percent
Whole pie	1/1	1.00	100%
Slice down the center	½	.50	50%
Slice each half (1/2) in half (1/2)	½ × ½ = ¼	.25	25%
Slice each quarter (1/4) in half (1/2)	¼ × ½ = ⅛	.125	12.5%

A whole pizza is sliced into 8 pieces. Each piece is, $\frac{1}{8}$, .125, or 12.5% of the whole pie.

FIGURE 3.2

Pizza Sliced

Photography by Thomas Myers

Conversion of a Proper Fraction to a Decimal

To convert a proper fraction to a decimal, divide the denominator into the numerator. The numerator is the dividend, and the denominator is the divisor. A calculator automatically inserts the decimal point. The decimal point represents the number is less than 1.

Table 3.1 displays a half-dollar as $\frac{1}{2}$, or .50 of $1.00.

$$\frac{1}{2} = .50$$

When you divide the numerator of 1 by the denominator of 2, the quotient is .50.

Conversion of a Decimal to a Percent

Table 3.1 displays a half-dollar as $\frac{1}{2}$, .50, and 50% of $1.00. To convert a decimal to a percentage, multiply the decimal by 100 and place the percent sign, %, to the right of the number.

$$.50 \times 100 = 50\%$$

When you are multiplying a decimal number by 100, you move the decimal point two places to the right.

QUICK TIP: You can convert a decimal to a percent by moving the decimal point two places to the right and adding a percent sign: .50 = 50%.

Conversion of a Percent to a Decimal

To convert a percent to a decimal, divide the percent by 100.

$$^{50\%}/_{100} = .50$$

When you are dividing the percent by 100, insert a decimal point two places to the left of the percent sign and remove the percent sign.

QUICK TIP: You can convert a percent to a decimal by moving the decimal point two places to the left of the percent sign and removing the percent sign.

Conversion of a Decimal to a Fraction

The conversion of a decimal to a fraction is simple. The decimal quantity becomes the numerator, and the decimal point is removed. The number of places beyond the decimal point determines the denominator. The denominator is limited to submultiples of 10.

$$0.4 = \frac{4}{10} \qquad 0.44 = \frac{44}{100} \qquad 0.444 = \frac{444}{1000}$$

Conclusion

Mixed numbers and noninteger quantities are very common in the professional kitchen. The majority of menu items served are a fraction, decimal, or percent of the total produced by the recipe. As food products are prepared, they become a fraction, decimal, or percent of their total purchased unit of measure. It is very important for your career to develop an understanding of the relationships between fractions, decimals, and percents.

Mixed Numbers and Noninteger Quantities: REVIEW PROBLEMS

Mixed Numbers

Convert the improper fractions that follow to mixed numbers. Use both methods: division and subtraction.

1. $\dfrac{6}{4}$

2. $\dfrac{10}{8}$

3. $\dfrac{12}{3}$

4. $\dfrac{4}{2}$

5. $\dfrac{7}{7}$

6. $\dfrac{100}{50}$

7. $\dfrac{28}{8}$

8. $\dfrac{15}{5}$

9. $\dfrac{20}{6}$

10. $\dfrac{22}{8}$

11. $\dfrac{18}{9}$

12. $\dfrac{10}{4}$

13. $\dfrac{16}{4}$

14. $\dfrac{40}{5}$

15. $\dfrac{12}{12}$

Fractions

Convert each fraction to a decimal and a percent.

1. $\dfrac{1}{2}$

2. $\dfrac{1}{4}$

3. $\dfrac{1}{3}$

4. $\dfrac{1}{5}$

5. $\dfrac{1}{6}$

6. $\dfrac{1}{8}$

7. $\dfrac{2}{5}$

8. $\dfrac{3}{5}$

9. $\dfrac{4}{5}$

10. $\dfrac{2}{3}$

11. $\dfrac{9}{10}$

12. $\dfrac{2}{4}$

13. $\dfrac{3}{4}$

14. $\dfrac{6}{10}$

15. $\dfrac{4}{8}$

Decimals

Convert each decimal to a percent and a fraction.

1. .10

2. .20

3. .15

4. .25

5. .33

6. .40

7. .80

8. 1.00

9. .50

10. .65

11. .66

12. .87

13. .99

14. .75

15. .45

Percents

Convert each percent to a decimal and a fraction.

1. 67%

2. 88%

3. 75%

4. 18%

5. 14%

6. 15%

7. 25%

8. 30%

9. 55%

10. 10%

11. 20%

12. 35%

13. 50%

14. 23%

15. 63%

Basic Mathematical Operations *with* Mixed Numbers *and* Noninteger Quantities

"The 2005 national survey of American Culinary programs report just over 90%, 9 out of 10, 0.90, or $\frac{9}{10}$ of programs offer scholarships.

—JOSEPH "MICK" LA LOPA, INSTRUCTOR AND WRITER, *CHEF EDUCATOR*

The basic mathematical operations of addition, subtraction, multiplication, and division apply to mixed numbers and noninteger quantities too. These basic operations are more complicated than they are with whole numbers. This chapter explains how to perform basic mathematical operations with mixed numbers and noninteger quantities.

LEARNING OBJECTIVES

1. To add, subtract, multiply, and divide fractions
2. To add, subtract, multiply, and divide mixed numbers
3. To add, subtract, multiply, and divide decimals
4. To multiply and divide percents

Fractions

PROPER FRACTIONS

Fractions are customarily reduced to their lowest term once any mathematical operation is completed. Reducing a fraction to its lowest term means the **greatest common factor** of the numerator and the denominator is 1. Reducing the fraction to its lowest term is done by dividing the numerator and the denominator by the greatest common factor that divides evenly into both of them. This produces a proper fraction. Remember, it is also customary to reduce an improper fraction to a mixed number.

To determine the greatest common factor of a fraction, you can use the test for divisibility. The test for divisibility to determine if a number is a multiple of a smaller number follows. A number is divisible by each of the following numbers if the adjacent conditions are satisfied.

TABLE 4.1   Test for Divisibility Chart

Divisible By The Number	If These Conditions Are Satisfied
2	If the last digit is an even number 2, 4, 6, 8 . . .
3	If the sum of the digits is divisible by 3: 12, 24, 60, 120 . . .
4	If the last two digits form a number that is divisible by 4: 12, 24, 60, 120 . . .
5	If the last digit is 0 or 5 60, 120, 420, 1,260 . . .
6	If the number is divisible by both 2 and 3 12, 24, 60, 120 . . .
7	If the division has no remainder: 420, 1,260 . . .
8	If the last three digits form a number divisible by 8: 24, 120, 1,260 . . .
9	If the sum of its digits is divisible by 9: 1,260 . . .
10	If the last digit is 0: 60, 120, 420, 1,260 . . .

QUICK TIP: The Math Facts Multiplication Grid in Appendix I can help you to find the greatest common factor of a fraction and fractions with and without common denominators.

ADDITION OF FRACTIONS WITH A COMMON DENOMINATOR

Adding fractions with a common denominator is simple. The numerators are added, and their sum is placed over the common denominator.

$$\frac{1}{8}+\frac{1}{8}+\frac{1}{8}+\frac{1}{8}=\frac{4}{8}$$

The sum, $\frac{4}{8}$, is reduced to its lowest terms by dividing the numerator and the denominator by their greatest common factor. The greatest common factor of both 4 and 8 is 4.

$$\frac{4}{8}=\frac{4/4}{8/4}=\frac{1}{2}$$

The proper fraction is $\frac{1}{2}$.

ADDITION OF FRACTIONS WITHOUT A COMMON DENOMINATOR

Fractions cannot be added unless they share a **common denominator**. A common denominator means all of the denominators in an equation are the same. A **least common denominator** is needed. The least common denominator is the **least common multiple** of the denominators of the fractions. The least common multiple of a group of numbers is the smallest number that is a multiple of each number in the group.

The following fraction equation has four denominators. The denominators are 2, 4, 8, and 16. A simple way to find the least common denominator is to list the multiples of each denominator.

| For the number 2: 2, 4, 6, 8, 10, 12, 14, 16 |
| For the number 4:   4,   8,   16 |
| For the number 8:   8,   16 |
| For the number 16:   16 |

$$\frac{1}{8}+\frac{3}{4}+\frac{1}{2}+\frac{5}{16}=$$

Sixteen is the number that is a multiple of all of the denominators. It is the least common denominator. Next, each numerator and denominator in the equation is multiplied by its respective **multiplier** to convert all of the denominators to 16.

The multiplier to convert 8 to 16 is 2. $\dfrac{1}{8} \times \dfrac{2}{2} = \dfrac{2}{16}$

The multiplier to convert 4 to 16 is 4. $\dfrac{3}{4} \times \dfrac{4}{4} = \dfrac{12}{16}$

The multiplier to convert 2 to 16 is 8. $\dfrac{1}{2} \times \dfrac{8}{8} = \dfrac{8}{16}$

The common denominator is 16; the sum of the fractions is as follows:

$$\dfrac{2}{16} + \dfrac{12}{16} + \dfrac{8}{16} + \dfrac{5}{16} = \dfrac{27}{16}$$

The improper fraction can be reduced to a mixed number by dividing the denominator into the numerator. If there is a remainder, it is written over the original denominator. With a standard calculator, the answer will be in decimal format. With long division, the answer will be a whole number with a remainder. This can also be done by subtracting the denominator from the numerator.

$$27 - 16 = 11$$

The answer from the subtraction exercise, 11, is the numerator in the mixed number.

$$^{27}\!/_{16} = 1.6875 \text{ or } 1\dfrac{11}{16}$$

The mixed number is $1\dfrac{11}{16}$.

SUBTRACTION OF FRACTIONS WITH A COMMON DENOMINATOR

Subtraction of fractions with a common denominator is simple too. Subtract the numerators and place the answer over the denominator.

$$\frac{7}{8} - \frac{5}{8} = \frac{2}{8}$$

The fraction, $\frac{2}{8}$, is then reduced to its lowest terms by dividing the numerator and the denominator by their greatest common factor. The greatest common factor of both 2 and 8 is 2.

$$\frac{2}{8} = \frac{2/2}{8/2} = \frac{1}{4}$$

The proper fraction is $\frac{1}{4}$.

SUBTRACTION OF FRACTIONS WITHOUT A COMMON DENOMINATOR

Fractions cannot be subtracted unless they share a common denominator. The process for finding a common denominator is the same as it is for addition of fractions. Once the equation has a common denominator, the numerators are subtracted. The answer is placed over the common denominator and reduced to its lowest terms. If the answer yields an improper fraction, it should be reduced to a mixed number.

MULTIPLICATION WITH FRACTIONS

Multiplying fractions is easy. The numerators are multiplied to find the numerator of the product. Then the denominators are multiplied to find the denominator of the product. If necessary, the product is reduced to a proper fraction.

$$\frac{2}{3} \times \frac{4}{9} = \frac{8}{27}$$

In this example, there is not a common factor for both 8 and 27, so the fraction cannot be reduced; $\frac{8}{27}$ is a proper fraction.

DIVISION WITH FRACTIONS

Division with fractions is almost as easy as multiplication, except the second fraction in the equation must be inverted, or turned over. This is called the **reciprocal**. Inverting the second fraction means the numerator and the denominator are switched. The numerator becomes the denominator, and the denominator becomes the numerator. Then you proceed as if you are multiplying the fractions.

$$\frac{3}{4} \div \frac{5}{6} = \frac{3}{4} \times \frac{6}{5} = \frac{18}{20}$$

In this example, $\frac{18}{20}$ must be reduced to a proper fraction. The number 2 is the greatest common factor of both 18 and 20.

$$\frac{18}{20} = \frac{18/2}{20/2} = \frac{9}{10}$$

The proper fraction is $\frac{9}{10}$.

Conclusion for Fractions

Performing basic mathematical operations with fractions requires special attention to the issues of common denominators, least common denominators, and least common multiples, and all answers must be reduced to a proper fraction or a mixed number.

Mathematical Operations Using Fractions: REVIEW PROBLEMS

Addition of Fractions with a Common Denominator

Reduce the sum of each problem to a proper fraction.

1. $\frac{1}{4} + \frac{1}{4} =$

2. $\frac{1}{3} + \frac{2}{3} =$

3. $\frac{5}{8} + \frac{7}{8} =$

4. $\frac{5}{9} + \frac{8}{9} =$

5. $\frac{1}{6} + \frac{3}{6} =$

6. $\frac{2}{7} + \frac{4}{7} =$

7. $\frac{15}{16} + \frac{6}{16} =$

8. $\frac{4}{9} + \frac{3}{9} =$

9. $\frac{1}{2} + \frac{1}{2} =$

10. $\frac{3}{4} + \frac{3}{4} =$

11. $\frac{2}{5} + \frac{3}{5} =$

12. $\frac{9}{14} + \frac{9}{14} =$

13. $\dfrac{12}{13}+\dfrac{11}{13}=$

15. $\dfrac{9}{11}+\dfrac{10}{11}=$

14. $\dfrac{7}{10}+\dfrac{9}{10}=$

Addition of Fractions without a Common Denominator

Reduce the sum of each problem to a proper fraction.

1. $\dfrac{1}{6}+\dfrac{2}{12}=$

9. $\dfrac{3}{10}+\dfrac{9}{30}=$

2. $\dfrac{3}{5}+\dfrac{8}{15}=$

10. $\dfrac{2}{7}+\dfrac{7}{21}=$

3. $\dfrac{1}{2}+\dfrac{3}{8}=$

11. $\dfrac{5}{12}+\dfrac{7}{24}=$

4. $\dfrac{1}{4}+\dfrac{1}{3}=$

12. $\dfrac{1}{2}+\dfrac{1}{8}=$

5. $\dfrac{4}{15}+\dfrac{1}{30}=$

13. $\dfrac{7}{18}+\dfrac{7}{9}=$

6. $\dfrac{1}{8}+\dfrac{3}{24}=$

14. $\dfrac{9}{11}+\dfrac{9}{22}=$

7. $\dfrac{9}{10}+\dfrac{11}{20}=$

15. $\dfrac{2}{15}+\dfrac{6}{45}=$

8. $\dfrac{1}{9}+\dfrac{5}{18}+$

Subtraction of Fractions with a Common Denominator

Reduce the difference of each problem to a proper fraction.

1. $\dfrac{5}{8}-\dfrac{1}{8}=$

5. $\dfrac{7}{13}-\dfrac{6}{13}=$

2. $\dfrac{7}{10}-\dfrac{5}{10}=$

6. $\dfrac{5}{9}-\dfrac{2}{9}=$

3. $\dfrac{3}{4}-\dfrac{1}{4}=$

7. $\dfrac{11}{12}-\dfrac{5}{12}=$

4. $\dfrac{2}{3}-\dfrac{1}{3}=$

8. $\dfrac{3}{24}-\dfrac{1}{24}=$

9. $\dfrac{6}{15} - \dfrac{1}{15} =$

13. $\dfrac{3}{18} - \dfrac{1}{18} =$

10. $\dfrac{13}{14} - \dfrac{9}{14} =$

14. $\dfrac{9}{14} - \dfrac{5}{14} =$

11. $\dfrac{9}{20} - \dfrac{7}{20} =$

15. $\dfrac{9}{22} - \dfrac{7}{22} =$

12. $\dfrac{15}{16} - \dfrac{5}{16} =$

Subtraction of Fractions without a Common Denominator

Reduce the difference of each problem to a proper fraction.

1. $\dfrac{1}{2} - \dfrac{1}{3} =$

9. $\dfrac{4}{5} - \dfrac{7}{20} =$

2. $\dfrac{2}{10} - \dfrac{1}{5} =$

10. $\dfrac{3}{8} - \dfrac{3}{16} =$

3. $\dfrac{3}{4} - \dfrac{5}{8} =$

11. $\dfrac{5}{6} - \dfrac{7}{9} =$

4. $\dfrac{1}{2} - \dfrac{1}{8} =$

12. $\dfrac{9}{20} - \dfrac{1}{5} =$

5. $\dfrac{2}{3} - \dfrac{1}{12} =$

13. $\dfrac{13}{20} - \dfrac{1}{2} =$

6. $\dfrac{3}{8} - \dfrac{1}{16} =$

14. $\dfrac{1}{2} - \dfrac{1}{4} =$

7. $\dfrac{1}{4} - \dfrac{1}{8} =$

15. $\dfrac{7}{8} - \dfrac{2}{3} =$

8. $\dfrac{11}{12} - \dfrac{19}{24} =$

Multiplication of Fractions

Reduce the product of each equation to a proper fraction.

1. $\dfrac{1}{2} \times \dfrac{1}{4} =$

2. $\dfrac{1}{4} \times \dfrac{1}{8} =$

3. $\dfrac{1}{3} \times \dfrac{1}{3} =$

4. $\dfrac{1}{2} \times \dfrac{1}{2} =$

5. $\dfrac{4}{5} \times \dfrac{1}{4} =$

6. $\dfrac{7}{8} \times \dfrac{7}{8} =$

7. $\dfrac{3}{4} \times \dfrac{1}{2} =$

8. $\dfrac{1}{6} \times \dfrac{1}{3} =$

9. $\dfrac{5}{6} \times \dfrac{6}{8} =$

10. $\dfrac{2}{7} \times \dfrac{1}{8} =$

11. $\dfrac{3}{4} \times \dfrac{2}{3} =$

12. $\dfrac{2}{3} \times \dfrac{1}{8} =$

13. $\dfrac{9}{10} \times \dfrac{1}{4} =$

14. $\dfrac{1}{5} \times \dfrac{1}{5} =$

15. $\dfrac{3}{4} \times \dfrac{5}{8} =$

Division of Fractions

Reduce the quotient of each equation to a proper fraction.

1. $\dfrac{1}{2} \div \dfrac{1}{2} =$

2. $\dfrac{4}{7} \div \dfrac{4}{7} =$

3. $\dfrac{1}{4} \div \dfrac{1}{2} =$

4. $\dfrac{5}{6} \div \dfrac{1}{6} =$

5. $\dfrac{2}{3} \div \dfrac{1}{3} =$

6. $\dfrac{9}{10} \div \dfrac{1}{10} =$

7. $\dfrac{6}{7} \div \dfrac{1}{3} =$

8. $\dfrac{1}{6} \div \dfrac{1}{4} =$

9. $\dfrac{3}{10} \div \dfrac{2}{5} =$

10. $\dfrac{4}{5} \div \dfrac{4}{5} =$

11. $\dfrac{5}{16} \div \dfrac{1}{8} =$

12. $\dfrac{5}{6} \div \dfrac{1}{6} =$

13. $\dfrac{11}{14} \div \dfrac{5}{14} =$

14. $\dfrac{6}{7} \div \dfrac{5}{8} =$

15. $\dfrac{1}{4} \div \dfrac{1}{8} =$

 **Mixed Numbers**

A **mixed number** is a whole number and a fraction. Basic mathematical operations with mixed numbers are the same as with fractions except the mixed number must first be changed to an improper fraction. When the mathematical operation is complete, the answer is reduced to the lowest terms. If the answer is an improper fraction, it is reduced to a mixed number.

CONVERTING A MIXED NUMBER TO AN IMPROPER FRACTION

A mixed number can be converted to an improper fraction by following these three steps.

> **STEP 1:** Multiply the denominator of the fraction by the whole-number portion.
>
> **STEP 2:** Add the numerator of the fraction to the product from Step 1.
>
> **STEP 3:** Write the sum over the original denominator.

The mixed number is $4\frac{1}{4}$.

STEP 1: In this example, the whole number, 4, is converted into fourths by multiplying the whole number, 4, by the denominator, 4. There are 16 fourths in the whole number 4.

$$4 \times 4 = 16$$

The number 16 becomes the numerator replacing the whole number while the denominator remains the number 4.

$$4 = \frac{16}{4}$$

STEP 2: The numerator of the mixed-number fraction, $\frac{1}{4}$, is added to the whole-number fraction, $\frac{16}{4}$, to produce the improper fration, $\frac{17}{4}$, used in the mathematical equation.

$$4 = \frac{16}{4}, + \frac{1}{4} = \frac{17}{4}$$

STEP 3: The mixed number, $4\frac{1}{4}$, equals $\frac{17}{4}$.

ADDITION OF MIXED NUMBERS WITH A COMMON DENOMINATOR

First, the mixed number is converted to an improper fraction with the same, or a common denominator, as the other fraction(s) in the equation. Then the numerators are added, and the sum is placed over the common denominator.

For the equation:

$$3\frac{1}{2} + \frac{1}{2} =$$

the mixed number, $3\frac{1}{2}$ is added to the fraction, $\frac{1}{2}$. The mixed number is first converted to an improper fraction, $\frac{7}{2}$. Then it is added to the fraction, $\frac{1}{2}$.

How does $3\frac{1}{2}$ become $\frac{7}{2}$?

The denominator, 2, is multiplied by the whole number, 3, to arrive at the number of $\frac{1}{2}$ in the number 3.

$$2 \times 3 = 6$$

There are six $\frac{1}{2}$s, in the number 3. The number 6 becomes the numerator for the number 3 as an improper fraction with a denominator of 2. The number 3 equals the improper fraction $\frac{6}{2}$.

Then, the numerator of $\frac{6}{2}$ is added to the numerator of $\frac{1}{2}$, for a total of $\frac{7}{2}$.

$$\frac{6}{2} + \frac{1}{2} = \frac{7}{2}$$

Now the equation can be added.

$$3\frac{1}{2} + \frac{1}{2} = \qquad \frac{7}{2} + \frac{1}{2} = \frac{8}{2}$$

The improper fraction $\frac{8}{2}$ is reduced to its lowest terms, the number 4.

$$\frac{8}{2} = \frac{8 \div 2}{2 \div 2} = \frac{4}{1} = 4$$

ADDITION OF MIXED NUMBERS WITHOUT A COMMON DENOMINATOR

In the previous example, the mixed number $3\frac{1}{2}$ was added to the fraction $\frac{1}{2}$. Both fractions in the equation had a common denominator of 2. If the denominators were not common, or the same, they would need to be converted to a least common denominator before the fractions could be added.

In the equation that follows, the mixed number $3\frac{1}{2}$ is being added to the fraction $\frac{1}{4}$. The mixed number $3\frac{1}{2}$ needs to be converted to an improper fraction with a denominator of 4.

$$3\frac{1}{2}+\frac{1}{4}=$$

The mixed number $3\frac{1}{2}$ is equal to $\frac{7}{2}$, but how many $\frac{1}{4}$ are in $\frac{1}{2}$?

By multiplying the fraction $\frac{7}{2}$ by the number 2, this improper fraction is converted into fourths.

$$\frac{7}{2}=\frac{7\times2}{2\times2}=\frac{14}{4}$$

The equation now has a common denominator of 4.

$$\frac{14}{4}+\frac{1}{4}=\frac{15}{4}$$

The improper fraction $\frac{15}{4}$ is reduced to a mixed number.

$$\frac{15}{4}=\frac{15\div4}{4\div4}=3\frac{3}{4}$$

The mixed number is $3\frac{3}{4}$.

SUBTRACTION OF MIXED NUMBERS WITH A COMMON DENOMINATOR

Subtraction with a mixed number follows the same rules as addition. The mixed number is converted to an improper fraction with the same, or common denominator as the other fraction in the equation. Then the numerators are subtracted and the difference is placed over the common denominator.

In the equation that follows, we are subtracting $\frac{1}{2}$ from $3\frac{1}{2}$. We have previously converted $3\frac{1}{2}$ to $\frac{7}{2}$, so the equation can be completed.

$$3\frac{1}{2}-\frac{1}{2}=\frac{7}{2}-\frac{1}{2}=\frac{6}{2}$$

The fraction, $\frac{6}{2}$, is an improper fraction.

$$\frac{6}{2} = \frac{6 \div 2}{2 \div 2} = \frac{3}{1} = 3$$

The answer is 3.

SUBTRACTION OF MIXED NUMBERS WITHOUT A COMMON DENOMINATOR

Subtraction can only occur between a mixed number and a fraction with a common denominator. Therefore, the mixed number is converted to an improper fraction with the same, or common, denominator as the other fraction in the equation.

MULTIPLICATION WITH MIXED NUMBERS

Multiplying a mixed number follows the same rules as multiplying any fractions. The mixed number is changed to an improper fraction. The numerators in the equation are multiplied to arrive at a product. Then the denominators in the equation are multiplied to arrive at a product. The product is reduced to its lowest terms.

$$3\frac{1}{2} \times \frac{1}{2} = \frac{7}{2} \times \frac{1}{2} = \frac{7}{4} = \frac{7 \div 4}{4 \div 4} = 1\frac{3}{4}$$

The mixed-number product for the equation is $1\frac{3}{4}$.

DIVISION WITH MIXED NUMBERS

Division with mixed numbers follows the same rules as division with fractions. The mixed number is converted to an improper fraction. The second fraction in the equation is inverted, or turned over. The numerators are multiplied to arrive at a product. Then the denominators are multiplied to arrive at a product. The product is reduced to its lowest terms.

$$3\frac{1}{2} \div \frac{1}{2} = \frac{7}{2} \times \frac{2}{1} = \frac{14}{2} = \frac{7}{1} = 7$$

The quotient is 7.

Conclusion for Mixed Numbers

The key to performing basic mathematical operations with mixed numbers is to convert the mixed numbers to improper fractions before the math is performed. Once the conversion to an improper fraction is complete, the rules for basic mathematics with fractions apply. When the equations are solved, the answer must again be converted to a mixed number or to a proper fraction.

Mixed Numbers:
REVIEW PROBLEMS

Convert these mixed numbers to an improper fraction

1. $4\dfrac{1}{8}$

2. $5\dfrac{1}{2}$

3. $1\dfrac{3}{8}$

4. $2\dfrac{3}{4}$

5. $3\dfrac{5}{8}$

6. $2\dfrac{2}{3}$

7. $5\dfrac{5}{6}$

8. $4\dfrac{1}{2}$

9. $8\dfrac{7}{8}$

10. $3\dfrac{1}{3}$

11. $1\dfrac{4}{5}$

12. $4\dfrac{5}{6}$

13. $2\dfrac{1}{4}$

14. $1\dfrac{1}{3}$

15. $5\dfrac{1}{5}$

Decimals

A **decimal** is a number written with a decimal point. A decimal is a noninteger quantity because it represents a number with a value less than (<) 1. Basic mathematical operations with decimals are similar to whole numbers, except a decimal point appears in the answers.

ADDITION WITH DECIMALS

Adding two or more decimal quantities is simple. The key is to line up the decimal points. The numbers are added, and the decimal point is inserted in the correct place in the sum.

$$
\begin{array}{r}
3.32 \\
6.48 \\
+\ 2.50 \\
\hline
12.30
\end{array}
$$

3.32 + 6.48 + 2.50 = 12.30

SUBTRACTION WITH DECIMALS

Subtraction with decimals is simple as well. The decimal points are lined up, and the numbers are subtracted. The decimal point appears in the answer.

$$
\begin{array}{r}
6.34 \\
-\ 3.23 \\
\hline
3.11
\end{array}
$$

6.34 − 3.23 = 3.11

MULTIPLICATION WITH DECIMALS

Multiplication with decimals is the same as multiplication with whole numbers, with one exception. Once the process is complete, the total number of decimal places in the equation are counted. The decimal point is inserted in the product, equal to the total number of decimal places in the equation.

$$
\begin{array}{r}
14.65 \text{ (two decimal spaces)} \\
\times\ .20 \text{ (two decimal spaces)} \\
\hline
2.9300 \text{ (four decimal spaces)}
\end{array}
$$

In this example, 14.65 is multiplied by .20. The product has four decimal spaces.

 **QUICK TIP:** Once the equation is solved, count the total number of decimal places in the equation. Next, count the total number of decimal places in the product and add the decimal point in the correct location. After this, the product can be rounded and any zeros from the product can be dropped.

DIVISION WITH DECIMALS

Division with decimals is the same as division with whole numbers, except the decimal point is inserted into the quotient. A calculator will automatically insert the decimal point into the quotient at the correct spot. If you are performing long division, the decimal point is moved over the same distance in both the divisor and the dividend. The decimal point is inserted in the quotient when the value is less than 1.

$$16.25\overline{)906.75} \text{ becomes } 1625\overline{)90675} \overset{55.80}{}$$

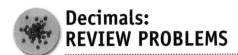

Decimals: REVIEW PROBLEMS

Addition with Decimals

1. 3.76
 + 2.99

2. 4.50
 + 6.33

3. 7.88
 + 9.25

4. 5.25
 + 6.00

5. 1.40
 + 5.66

6. 4.89
 + 1.30

7. 9.99
 + 7.89

8. 8.65
 + 6.25

9. 3.30
 + 4.55

10. 4.44
 + 6.66

11. 7.75
 + 6.75

12. 8.00
 + 6.00

13. 25.01
       + 10.50
       ‾‾‾‾‾‾‾

15. 30.00
       + 15.15
       ‾‾‾‾‾‾‾

14. 12.45
       + 14.85
       ‾‾‾‾‾‾‾

Subtraction with Decimals

1. 10.00
      − 8.45
      ‾‾‾‾‾‾

9. 21.75
      − 10.50
      ‾‾‾‾‾‾‾

2. 9.99
      − 8.88
      ‾‾‾‾‾‾

10. 16.90
       − 5.95
       ‾‾‾‾‾‾

3. 45.45
      − 30.00
      ‾‾‾‾‾‾‾

11. 900.33
       − 876.42
       ‾‾‾‾‾‾‾‾

4. 50.00
      − 33.33
      ‾‾‾‾‾‾‾

12. 12.25
       − 11.50
       ‾‾‾‾‾‾‾

5. 23.35
      − 12.50
      ‾‾‾‾‾‾‾

13. 18.99
       − 15.55
       ‾‾‾‾‾‾‾

6. 36.25
      − 14.89
      ‾‾‾‾‾‾‾

14. 35.86
       − 14.84
       ‾‾‾‾‾‾‾

7. 15.15
      − 8.90
      ‾‾‾‾‾‾

15. 1,015.33
       − 850.39
       ‾‾‾‾‾‾‾‾

8. 14.00
      − 12.95
      ‾‾‾‾‾‾

Multiplication with Decimals

1. 32.32
  × 1.34

2. 12.65
  × 2.00

3.   3.60
  × .40

4.   4.44
  × 2.22

5.   4.50
  × .01

6. 420.00
  × 10.00

7.   6.75
  × 2.25

8.   .87
  × 1.00

9.   2.22
  × .5

10. 1.25
  × .2

Division with Decimals

1. 1.39 ÷ .67

2. 2.89 ÷ .80

3. 3.59 ÷ 45

4. 2.59 ÷ .62

5. $\dfrac{2.50}{.20}$

6. $\dfrac{3.35}{.35}$

7. $\dfrac{5.99}{.80}$

8. $\dfrac{8.99}{.60}$

9. $4.55/.50$

10. $2.99/.50$

11. $.99/.62$

12. $2.50/.89$

13. $.56\overline{)8.67}$

14. $1.25\overline{)6.99}$

15. $.25\overline{)1.00}$ **16.** $.40\overline{)3.95}$

Percents

Basic mathematical operations can be performed with percents, although it is common for the percent to be converted to a decimal. Some find it easier to perform basic mathematical operations with decimals. If the answer requires a percent, the decimal can easily be converted to a percent. Percents are very common in foodservice operations.

MULTIPLICATION WITH PERCENTS

Multiplication with a percent is similar to multiplication with whole numbers or numbers with a decimal. Converting the percent to a decimal produces the same product.

$$2 \times 50\% = 1 \text{ or } 2 \times .50 = 1.00 \text{ or } 1$$

DIVISION WITH PERCENTS

Division with a percent is also similar to division with whole numbers or numbers with a decimal. Converting the percent to a decimal produces the same quotient.

$$\frac{2}{50\%} = 4 \qquad 2\big/50\% = 4 \qquad 2 \div 50\% = 4 \qquad 50\%\overline{)2}^{\,4}$$

or

$$\frac{2}{.50} = 4 \qquad 2\big/.50 = 4 \qquad 2 \div .50 = 4 \qquad .50\overline{)2}^{\,4}$$

Conclusion

Basic mathematics with mixed numbers and noninteger quantities requires more attention than mathematics with whole numbers. There are special rules for basic mathematics with fractions, decimals, and percents. Mixed numbers and noninteger quantities are very common in foodservice mathematics. You may need to review this chapter often.

CHAPTER **5**

Basic Mathematics: Additional Information *and* Tips *for* Success

"Math is a four-letter word."

—JOSEPH "MICK" LA LOPA, INSTRUCTOR AND WRITER, *CHEF EDUCATOR*

There are mathematical terms and symbols that can help you with the concepts in foodservice mathematics. The terms are rounding and estimation, multipliers or conversion factors, ratios and proportions. The symbols are ">" for greater than and "<" for less than. These terms and symbols are explained in this chapter. They will help you as you progress through the text.

LEARNING OBJECTIVES

1. To review mathematical terminology used in the foodservice industry, including the following:

   a. Rounding and estimation

   b. Multipliers and conversion factors

   c. Ratios

   d. Proportions

2. To review the symbols for ">" (greater than) and for "<" (less than)

Rounding and Estimation

Rounding is the expression of numbers to the nearest hundred, to the nearest thousand, or to a specific number of significant digits. **Significant digits** are nonzero digits. The general rule for rounding a number to a nonzero digit is to locate the leftmost digit. This digit is the rounding place. Then examine the digit to the immediate right.

If the digit to the right of the rounding place is 0, 1, 2, 3, or 4, do not change the digit in the rounding place. If the digit to the right of the rounding place is 5, 6, 7, 8, or 9, add 1 to the digit in the rounding place.

> The number 65.5 can be rounded *up* to 66.
>
> The number 65.56 can be rounded *up* to 65.6.
>
> The number 65.567 can be rounded *up* to 65.57.
>
> The number 65.5678 can be rounded *up* to 65.568.

> The number 65.4 can be rounded *down* to 65.
>
> The number 65.43 can be rounded *down* to 65.4.
>
> The number 65.433 can be rounded *down* to 65.43.
>
> The number 65.4332 can be rounded *down* to 65.433.

> With a repeating decimal or a recurring decimal:
>
> .3333 = .34   and   .6666 = .67

 The last digit can be represented by a whole number, decimal, fraction, or a percent. The rules for rounding apply to all of these representations.

Rounding should occur *after* a calculation is completed. In some foodservice situations, the numbers in the equation will be carried out to four decimal places. After the calculations, a decision should be made regarding how many decimal places the answer should be rounded to. If the rounding decision is incorrect, it can cause a mathematical error.

In a real-life foodservice operation, a server may drop a plate, and a line cook may burn a steak. A safety level or margin of error should be considered when rounding for foodservice situations. *The rule of thumb is to round up when an adequate amount of product is required.* The product may be food, beverage, linen, china, glass, and so on.

Another foodservice situation where rounding "incorrectly" can negatively impact the outcome is when the cost of a menu item, or a menu price, is being calculated. If the cost of an item is rounded down, the result may be a menu price that is too low. If this menu item is popular, the little bit of money lost due to rounding incorrectly, becomes a lot of money lost due to the sales volume of the menu item. Good judgment is required when rounding for the foodservice industry.

Estimate means to make an opinion or judgment about the mathematical value of an item. You can estimate the length of a banquet table to determine the correct-size tablecloth. You can estimate the number of portions of a menu item that will be sold tonight so you can prepare the correct amount of food. In the introduction to this book, the vice president of a company estimated the number of portions of crab legs the average guest would eat.

Estimating is a tool that can save you time. However, before you make an estimate, make sure you have all of the information available to help you to make an educated decision. In the previous discussion on rounding for real-life situations, the process of estimating plays a role. Remember, an incorrect estimate can have an impact on your customers, the employees, and your profit.

Multiplier or Conversion Factor

A **multiplier** or a **conversion factor** is a number used to multiply by. It represents a relationship that is constant—a relationship that does not change. The use of a multiplier or a conversion factor in foodservice is very common. The conversion of a recipe's ingredients and cost between the standard and metric system can be achieved by using a multiplier. The yield of a recipe is changed with the use of a conversion factor. The process for using a multiplier will be introduced in the next section of this text.

Ratios

A **ratio** is the indicated quotient of two mathematical expressions. It expresses the relationship in quantity, amount, or size between two or more numbers. Ratios are very common in the professional kitchen and the professional bake shop for basic recipes.

The basic recipe for stock uses a ratio of 1 gallon of water to 1 pound of mirepoix. The recipe for mirepoix uses a ratio of 2 parts onion to 1 part celery to 1 part carrot (2 to 1 to 1, or 2:1:1). This ratio for mirepoix means the weight of the onions is always twice the weight of the celery and carrots. The celery and the carrot are equal in weight, and they are one-half the weight of the onion.

How do you determine the weight of the onion, celery, and carrots using the ratio of 2 to 1 to 1? The four steps to solving a ratio are as follows:

> **STEP 1.** Add the total number of parts in the ratio.
>
> **STEP 2.** Determine the total quantity of product to produce.
>
> **STEP 3.** Divide the total quantity of product to produce (Step 2) by the total number of parts in the ratio (Step 1).
>
> **STEP 4.** Multiply each part in the ratio by the amount determined in Step 3.

So, for the example, you perform the following steps:

STEP 1.   Add the total number of parts in the ratio.

In this ratio, 2 to 1 to 1, the total number of parts is 4: 2 + 1 + 1 = 4.

STEP 2.   Determine the total quantity of product to produce.

The basic recipe for stock lists 1 gallon of water to 1 pound of mirepoix. One pound of mirepoix is the amount of product needed.

STEP 3.   Divide the total quantity of product to produce (Step 2) by the total number of parts in the ratio (Step 1).

> 1 pound divided by 4 equals: 1 pound ÷ 4 (parts) = .25 pounds
>
> or
>
> 16 ounces ÷ 4 (parts) = 4 ounces

Each part of the ratio is equal to .25 of a pound, or 4 ounces.

STEP 4:   Multiply each part in the ratio by the amount determined in Step 3.

> Onions: 2 parts × .25 pound = .5 pound; or 2 parts × 4 ounces = 8 ounces onion
>
> Celery: 1 part × .25 = .25 pound celery; or 1 part × 4 ounces = 4 ounces celery
>
> Carrot: 1 part × .25 = .25 pound carrot; or 1 part × 4 ounces = 4 ounces carrot

The amount of mirepoix needed to make 1 gallon of stock is 1 pound. This 1 pound consists of .5 pound or 8 ounces onion, .25 pound or 4 ounces celery, and .25 pound or 4 ounces carrot.

Proportions

A **proportion** expresses the relation of one part to another or to the whole with respect to quantity. A proportion expresses a consistent ratio. Proportion is used in foodservice when the amount of an ingredient in a basic "ratio" recipe is unknown.

The basic recipe for white bread is 12 ounces of water to 20 ounces of bread flour. This recipe produces one loaf of white bread. If I have 80 ounces of flour, how much water do I need to use to produce 4 loaves of white bread?

The three steps to solving a proportion are as follows:

> **STEP 1:** Set up the proportion.
>
> **STEP 2:** Isolate x. There are two methods to isolate x, as described below.
>
> **STEP 3:** Solve for x.

So, for the example, you perform the following steps:

STEP 1: Set up the proportion.

A proportion can solve for the amount of water needed. The proportion is set up as a ratio fraction, using the known quantities and solving for the unknown, x.

This proportion is $\frac{12}{20} = \frac{x}{80}$, where 12 ounces of water are needed for 20 ounces of bread flour and x ounces of water are needed for 80 ounces of bread flour.

STEP 2 (Method 1): Isolate x. This can be done in one of two ways. The first method was introduced in Chapter 4 as dividing fractions, which becomes multiplication.

This process inverts the second fraction before you multiply the numerators and the denominators:

$$\frac{12}{20} = \frac{x}{80} \text{ becomes } \frac{12}{20} \times \frac{80}{x}$$

Multiplication produces $960 = 20\,x$.

STEP 2 (Method 2): The standard method for solving a proportion is to cross multiply the numerators and the denominators. This process isolates x and produces the same answer.

$$\frac{12}{20} = \frac{x}{80} \text{ becomes } \frac{12}{20} \diagtimes \frac{x}{80}$$

Cross multiplication produces the equation $20x = 960$.

STEP 3: Solve for x.

Each side of the equation is divided by 20 to isolate x.

$$960 \div 20 = 48 \text{ and } 20x \div 20 = x.$$
$$x = 48$$

48 ounces of water are needed for 80 ounces of bread flour. This will produce 4 loaves of white bread.

Greater Than (>) and Less Than (<)

> The > symbol means greater than. For instance, the number 20 > 10.
> The < symbol means less than. For instance, the number 10 < 20.

These symbols explain the relationship of one number to another.

QUICK TIP: The addition of two or more numbers yields a sum greater than (>) the numbers in the equation.

$$10 + 10 = 20, 20 > 10$$

QUICK TIP: The subtraction of one number from another yields an answer less than (<) the numbers in the equation.

$$20 - 15 = 5, 5 < 20 \text{ and } 15$$

QUICK TIP: Multiplication with any numbers greater than (>) 1 yields a product greater than (>) the numbers in the equation.

$$10 \times 2 = 20, 20 > 10 \text{ or } 2$$

QUICK TIP: Multiplication with any number less than (<) 1 (fraction, decimal, or percent) yields a product less than (<) the whole number in the equation.

$$10 \times \text{(either) } \tfrac{1}{2}, .50, \text{ or } 50\% = 5, 5 < 10$$

QUICK TIP: Division with a number greater than (>)1 yields a quotient smaller than the numbers in the equation.

$$20 \div 2 = 10, 10 < 20$$

QUICK TIP: Division with a number less than (<) 1 yields a quotient larger than the numbers in the equation.

$$20 \div \text{(either) } \tfrac{1}{2}, .50, \text{ or } 50\% = 40, 40 < 20$$

These Quick Tips can help you determine if your math is correct.

Conclusion

Mathematical terminology and symbols are commonly used in the culinary arts and foodservice industry. The terms are rounding and estimation, multiplier and conversion factor, ratio, and proportion. The symbols are > for greater than and < for less than. Understanding these terms and symbols will aid in your understanding of mathematics for foodservice.

Basic Mathematics and Additional Tips: REVIEW PROBLEMS

Rounding and Estimation

Round up or down to make the following quantities whole numbers.

1. 5.34

2. 7.6

3. 132.667

4. 44.50

5. 89.998

6. 22.45

7. 101.112

8. 254.443

9. 97.65

10. 2,204.33

11. 3,330.97

12. 10,000.6

Estimate the number of the items needed using the scenario that follows.

The Best in the West Boutique Hotel serves dinner on Friday and Saturday nights. The number of reservations for dinner is usually 50% of the total number of meals served in the restaurant. The number of guests that order the special of the night is 30% of the number of reservations. The number of guests that order dessert is 100% of the number of reservations. The number of guests that order a prime rib dinner is 20% of the number of reservations.

If 90 guests have made a reservation for dinner tonight:

1. How many guests should the restaurant serve tonight?

2. How many guests will order the special tonight?

3. How many guests will order dessert tonight?

4. How many guests will order the prime rib dinner tonight?

Write a short paragraph to explain how you estimated your answers to Questions 1 to 4.

Ratios

Use the four-step method to solve the following ratio problems.

1. A basic vinaigrette dressing uses a ratio of 3 parts oil to 1 part vinegar. The garde manger chef expects you to produce 2 gallons of vinaigrette. What quantity of oil and vinegar will you use to produce 2 gallons of vinaigrette?

STEP 1: Add the total number of parts in the ratio.

STEP 2: Determine the total quantity of product to produce.

STEP 3: Divide the total quantity of product to produce (Step 2) by the total number of parts in the ratio (Step 1).

STEP 4: Multiply each part in the ratio by the amount determined in Step 3.

2. The basic recipe for a vegetable salad is 4 parts tomato, 3 parts asparagus, 2 parts avocado, and 1 part cucumber. The garde manger chef expects you to produce 20 pounds of this salad. What quantity of each ingredient will you need to produce 20 pounds of salad?

STEP 1: Add the total number of parts in the ratio.

STEP 2: Determine the total quantity of product to produce.

STEP 3: Divide the total quantity of product to produce (Step 2) by the number of parts in the ratio (Step 1).

STEP 4: Multiply each part in the ratio by the amount determined in Step 3.

3. The basic recipe for a chicken salad is 5 parts chicken, 2 parts mayonnaise, 2 parts celery, and 1 part almonds. The garde manger chef expects you to produce 10 pounds of chicken salad. What quantity of each ingredient will you need to produce 10 pounds of chicken salad?

STEP 1:   **Add the total number of parts in the ratio.**

STEP 2:   **Determine the total amount of product to produce.**

STEP 3:   **Divide the total amount of product to produce (Step 2) by the number of parts in the ratio (Step 1).**

STEP 4:   **Multiply each part in the ratio by the amount determined in Step 3.**

Proportions

Use the three-step method to solve the following proportion problems.

1. The recipe for cookie dough is 42 ounces of flour to 16 ounces of sugar. You have 210 ounces of flour. How many ounces of sugar do you need to make this cookie dough recipe using all of the flour you have?

STEP 1:   **Set up the proportion.**

STEP 2:   **Isolate x.**

STEP 3:   **Solve for x.**

2. The recipe for pie crust uses 12 ounces of flour and 4 ounces of butter. If you have 24 ounces of butter, how much flour do you need to use all of the butter?

STEP 1:   **Set up the proportion.**

STEP 2:   **Isolate x.**

STEP 3:   **Solve for x.**

3. The recipe for ice cream uses 32 fluid ounces of cream for every 1 pound of sugar. If you have 12 pounds of sugar, how much cream do you need to make this ice cream recipe?

STEP 1: Set up the proportion.

STEP 2: Isolate *x*.

STEP 3: Solve for *x*.

MATHEMATICS
for the
PROFESSIONAL
KITCHEN

CHAPTER 6

The Standardized Recipe

"The standardized recipe is the foundation of the modern American foodservice industry. These recipes are the most important documents to ensure a profitable business."

—TERRI JONES

The standardized recipe is the hallmark of the foodservice industry today. The information contained in the standardized recipe ensures that a consistent product is always served to the guest. A consistent product means the look, taste, texture, and portion size of the menu item is the same each time the item is prepared and served, regardless of who is in the kitchen on a given day.

Each standardized recipe has a specific yield, which can be increased or decreased as needed. The recipe's yield is used to determine the cost per portion to serve the item to your guests. The portion cost is then used to develop the menu or sales price. This is the basis of a good cost control program. The standardized recipe is a vital part of the profitable foodservice operation.

 LEARNING OBJECTIVES

1. To understand the format for a standardized recipe
2. To understand the content of the standardized recipe
3. To recognize the importance of the standardized recipe
4. To understand the yield of a recipe
5. To understand how to increase or decrease the yield of a recipe
6. To write your own standardized recipes for use in your case study

Standardized Recipe Format

A standardized recipe contains a variety of information about the recipe, its yield, and the number of portions it produces. The actual form may vary from one operation to another, but the information contained is the same. The following is an example of a standardized recipe form.

STANDARDIZED RECIPE FORM

Item Name

Preparation and Cooking Time: **Recipe Yield:**
Portion Size: **Number of Portions:**

Quantity	Ingredients	Preparation Method
Ingredient quantities are listed in a specific unit of measure. The units are either weight, volume, or count. An example of weight is pounds, volume is gallons, and count is a number, such as 3 eggs. Units of measure are detailed in Chapter 7.	Ingredients are listed in the order that they are added to the recipe. The item added first is at the top of the list, then the second item, and so on.	This column describes the exact method of preparation for each ingredient as it is added to the recipe. For example, ingredient one might be sautéed, before ingredient two is added. After all ingredients are added, the entire mixture might be simmered.

The Importance of the Standardized Recipe

The standardized recipe is the key to success in the foodservice industry. This simple form offers the foodservice operation ALL of the information needed for success. The standardized recipe form identifies the type or style of food, the food products to purchase, the equipment needed to prepare the food, the yield of the recipe, and the skill level of the employees.

The cost to purchase the food determines the **cost per portion**, which is directly related to the menu price. The menu price and the guests' perception of its value are crucial to the success of the restaurant.

Recipe Yield and Recipe Conversion

RECIPE YIELD

Recipe yield refers to the total weight, volume, count, or number of portions a properly prepared recipe produces. This information is critical to production planning. In the example that follows, the recipe for soup yields 2 gallons of soup. This yield is for illustrative purposes only.

In the professional kitchen, a recipe for soup with a yield of 2 gallons would have an actual yield of 95%, or 1.9 gallons of soup. That is the total amount of soup that could be served to a guest because some of the soup would stick to the side of the stock pot. This concept, called edible portion or as served quantity, is covered in Chapter 8.

RECIPE YIELD EXAMPLE

The recipe for soup yields 2 gallons.

The portion size for soup is 8 fl. oz.

2 (gallons) × 128 (fl. oz. per gallons) = 256 fl. oz. of soup

The recipe yields a total of 256 fl. oz.

256 (fl. oz. of soup) ÷ 8 (fl. oz. portion size) = 32 total portions for 2 gallons

The recipe yields 32 portions of 8 fl. oz. each.

RECIPE CONVERSIONS

A recipe's yield may need to be increased or decreased depending on the number of portions required to serve guests. *Adjusting a recipe's yield impacts the quantity of all the recipe's ingredients equally.* (Extra caution should be exercised when adjusting the quantities for herbs, spices, and seasonings.) The process of adjusting the yield of a recipe is simple. It is based on the concept of a conversion factor.

The formula for recipe conversion is as follows:

$$\frac{\text{New yield}}{\text{Old yield}} = \text{Conversion factor}$$

The conversion factor is used to multiply the quantity of all of the recipe's ingredients.

RECIPE CONVERSION EXAMPLE

Recipe A yields 25 portions.

The banquet chef is serving 100 portions of Recipe A on Saturday.

The new yield is 100. The old yield is 25.

$$\frac{100 \text{ (new yield)}}{25 \text{ (old yield)}} = 4 \text{ (conversion factor)}$$

The number 4, the conversion factor, is multiplied by the quantity listed for each of the ingredients in the recipe to increase the yield, or number of portions, produced from Recipe A.

Recipe A: Yields 25

Item	Quantity
Potatoes	5 pounds

Recipe A: Yield 100

Item	Quantity
Potatoes	5 (pounds) × 4 (conversion factor) = 20 pounds

The quantity of potatoes to serve 100 portions is 20 pounds.

 Conclusion

The standardized recipe is the key to a successful foodservice operation. The recipe contains all of the information needed to purchase food and prepare the menu items. Each standardized recipe has a yield, or a number of portions it produces. The yield of a standardized recipe can be increased or decreased using a conversion factor. The new yield can be larger or smaller than the original yield.

 **The Standardized Recipe:
REVIEW PROBLEMS**

Determine the conversion factor used to adjust the yield for the following recipes.

$$\frac{\text{New yield}}{\text{Old yield}} = \text{Conversion factor}$$

Recipe	New Yield	Old Yield	Multiplier
A	60	30	
B	200	100	
C	30	60	
D	50	100	
E	50	200	
F	150	25	
G	70	150	
H	45	20	
I	500	25	
J	15	60	

Running Case Study

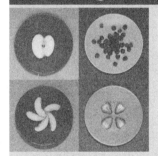

Steps I and II—Standardized Recipes

This is the beginning of the running case study in this textbook. Step I is to convert three recipes into the standardized recipe format. Step II is to adjust the yield of the three recipes so each one serves 50 portions.

The recipes will be used in later chapters to illustrate how to adjust a recipe to its correct units of measure, to cost a recipe, to cost a portion, and to price an item on a menu.

RUNNING CASE STUDY

Thomas Morgan is a culinary student whose goal is to open *Tomas,* an Italian restaurant. Thomas realizes that the first step in the process is to gather recipes for his entrée items. Recipe 1 is a family secret for meatballs. Recipes 2 and 3 are from his favorite Italian cookbook. Thomas has placed his three recipes into the standardized recipe format. For this exercise, it is only necessary to list the quantity and the ingredients. The preparation column is left blank. (This book does not cover food preparation.)

Next, Thomas will determine the conversion factor to increase the yield of the recipe, or the number of portions the recipe will yield to 50. Then he will multiply all of his ingredients by the multiplier. In the next section of the running case study in Chapter 7, Thomas will adjust his ingredients to their correct unit of measure.

Standardized Recipe #1

The Best Meatballs Ever

Preparation and Cooking Time: 1.5 hours   **Recipe Yield: 60 Each**
Portion Size: 2 each   **Number of Portions: 30**

Quantity	Ingredients	Preparation Method
5 pounds	Ground beef	
5 pounds	Ground pork	
10 cups	Italian bread crumbs	
10 each	Eggs	
	Recipe served 30 portions.	
	To serve 50 portions:	
	New/Old = Conversion factor	
	50/30 = 1.6666, rounded to 1.67	
5 pounds × 1.67 = 8.3 pounds	Ground beef	
5 pounds × 1.67 = 8.3 pounds	Ground pork	
10 cups × 1.67 = 16.7 cups	Italian bread crumbs	
10 eggs × 1.67 = 16.7	Eggs	

Standardized Recipe #2

Beef Braised in Red Wine Sauce

Preparation and Cooking Time: 3.5 hours
Portion Size:

Recipe Yield:
Number of Portions: 6

Quantity	Ingredients	Preparation Method
2 T	Vegetable oil	
4 pounds	Beef roast	
1 T	Butter	
3 T	Yellow onion, chopped	
2 T	Carrot, chopped	
2 T	Celery, chopped	
1.5 cups	Dry red wine	
1 cup	Beef stock	
1.5 T	Italian tomatoes	
Pinch	Thyme	
1/8 tsp.	Marjoram	
	Recipe served 6 portions.	
	To serve 50 portions:	
	New/Old = Conversion factor	
	50/6 = 8.3333, rounded to 8.3	
2 T × 8.3 = 16.67 T	Vegetable oil	
4 pounds × 8.3 = 33.2 pounds	Beef roast	
1 T × 8.3 = 8.3 T	Butter	
3 T × 8.3 = 24.9 T (25 T)	Yellow onion, chopped	
2 T × 8.3 = 16.6 T	Carrot, chopped	
2 T × 8.3 = 16.6 T	Celery, chopped	
1.5 cups × 8.3 = 12.5 cups	Dry red wine	
1 cup × 8.3 = 8.3 cups	Beef stock	
1.5 T × 8.3 = 12.5 T	Italian tomatoes	
Pinch × 8.3 = 0.5 tsp.	Thyme	
1/8 tsp. × 8.3 = 1 tsp.	Majoram	

Standardized Recipe #3

Veal Scaloppine with Lemon Sauce

Preparation and Cooking Time: 5 min.
Portion Size: .25 pound

Recipe Yield:
Number of Portions: 4

Quantity	Ingredients	Preparation Method
2 T	Vegetable oil	
1/4 cup	Butter	
1 pound	Veal, pounded flat	
3/4 cup	Flour	
2 T	Lemon juice	
2 T	Parsley, chopped	
1/2	Lemon, sliced	
	Recipe served 4 portions.	
	To serve 50 portions:	
	New/Old = Conversion factor	
	50/4 = 12.5	
2 T × 12.5 = 25 T	Vegetable oil	
1/4 cup × 12.5 = 3.125 cups	Butter	
1 pound × 12.5 = 12.5 pounds	Veal, pounded flat	
3/4 cup × 12.5 = 9.375 cup	Flour	
2 T × 12.5 = 25 T	Lemon juice	
2 T × 12.5 = 25 T	Parsley, chopped	
1/2 × 12.5 = 6.25	Lemon, sliced	

REVIEW PROBLEMS: THE STANDARDIZED RECIPE

STEP I: Fill in three standardized recipe forms with your favorite recipes. They can be family secrets, from your favorite cookbook, magazines, or from a dish you've created.

STEP II: Determine the conversion factor to serve 50 portions, and convert the quantities of each ingredient to ensure that, when combined, they will yield 50 portions.

STANDARDIZED RECIPE 1

Preparation and Cooking Time: Recipe Yield:
Portion Size: Number of Portions:

Quantity   Ingredients   Preparation Method

STANDARDIZED RECIPE 2

Preparation and Cooking Time: **Recipe Yield:**
Portion Size: **Number of Portions:**

Quantity	Ingredients	Preparation Method

STANDARDIZED RECIPE 3

Preparation and Cooking Time: **Recipe Yield:**
Portion Size: **Number of Portions:**

Quantity	Ingredients	Preparation Method

CHAPTER 7

Units *of* Measure

*"Consistency of product, taste, and portion size are the greatest
challenges to the foodservice operator.
Consistency is impossible without the correct units of measure."*

—TERRI JONES

The standardized recipe is the map or tool that is used in the professional kitchen to take you from the *mise en place,* the setting up of tools and ingredients to begin cooking, to the finished product. This tool must be used correctly in order to achieve success. Success begins with the accurate measurement of the ingredients in the recipe.

LEARNING OBJECTIVES

1. To identify the U.S. standard units of measure for volume
2. To list the measuring devices used for liquids
3. To identify the U.S. standard units of measure for weight
4. To understand the different scales used for weight
5. To understand the difference between a fluid ounce and a weight ounce
6. To identify the metric system units of measure for volume
7. To list the metric system units of measure for weight
8. To master the conversion of U.S. standard units of measure to the metric system

U.S. Standard Units of Measure

VOLUME UNITS OF MEASURE

Liquids are measured by volume. Liquids include water, juice, oil, stock, or other liquids with waterlike consistency. Volume units of measure include gallon, quart, pint, cup, fluid ounce, tablespoon, and teaspoon. The relationship among these volume units of measure is displayed in Table 7.1

VOLUME MEASURING TOOLS

Properly measuring the liquids used in a standardized recipe ensures the production of a consistent menu item. Volume containers are placed on a flat surface and filled to the desired level. The basic measuring tools are containers that can hold a range of liquid volumes, from one cup to one gallon, along with measuring spoons of various measurements.

Volume measuring tools are also used to portion some foods for service to guests. Portioning foods also requires accurate measurements because the menu price is based on a certain-size portion. Sauces and soups are liquid items portioned using ladles. A ladle is a common tool used to measure liquids. Ladles are available in sizes ranging from a ½ fluid ounce (fl. oz.) to 32 fluid ounces. Common ladle sizes used for portioning are ½ fl. oz., 1 fl. oz., 2 fl. oz., 3 fl. oz., 6 fl. oz., and 8 fl. oz. Larger-sized ladles are used in the cooking process, not as a tool for portion control.

Bowls, crocks, cups, and monkey dishes are used as portion-control tools for liquid items. A bowl will only hold so many fluid ounces of soup. If more

TABLE 7.1 U.S. Volume Units of Measure and Their Equivalents

Gallon (G, gal)	Quart (qt)	Pint (pt)	Cup (C, c)	Fluid Ounce (fl. oz.)	Tablespoon (T, tbsp.)	Teaspoon (t, tsp.)
1 gallon	4 quarts	8 pints	16 cups	128 fl. oz.		
½ gallon	2 quarts	4 pints	8 cups	64 fl. oz.		
	1 quart	2 pints	4 cups	32 fl. oz.		
		1 pint	2 cups	16 fl. oz.		
			1 cup	8 fl. oz.	16 T	
			½ cup	4 fl. oz.	8 T	
			¼ cup	2 fl. oz.	4 T	
				1 fl. oz.	2 T	
					1 T	3 tsp.

FIGURE 7.1

U.S. Volume Units of Measure: One gallon, half gallon, one quart, one pint.

Photography by Thomas Myers

FIGURE 7.2

U.S. Volume Units of Measure: Tablespoon, teaspoon, and partial units of a teaspoon.

Photography by Thomas Myers

FIGURE 7.3

Nested ladles: 32 ounces to 1 ounce.

Photography by Thomas Myers

FIGURE 7.4

Bowls, a cup, and a crock.

Photography by Thomas Myers

soup is put into the bowl than its volume can hold, the soup is wasted. The same is true for crocks, cups, and monkey dishes.

Dishers/scoops are another volume unit of measure commonly used as a portion-control tool. Dishers/scoops come in a variety of sizes, from a number 60, which is equal to $\frac{1}{2}$ fl. oz., to a number 6, which is equal to 5.33 fl. oz., or $\frac{2}{3}$ of a cup. The disher/scoop size is based on the number of scoops you can serve from 1 quart, a quart being a volume unit of measure. The disher/scoop is often used for frozen desserts, such as ice cream or sorbet. These items are liquid before they are frozen, so a volume measuring tool is used.

FIGURE 7.5

Dishers/scoops: Sizes (from left to right) 10, 24, 30, and 40.
Photography by Thomas Myers

The disher/scoop is also used to portion food items that are not liquid or measured by volume. Mashed potatoes and tuna salad are examples of food items not liquid in nature that are often portioned with the disher/scoop. These items can also be weighted.

TABLE 7.2 Size and Capacity of Dishers/Scoops

Number on Disher/Scoop	Volume Measure
6	3¼ tsp.
8	3¾ tsp.
10	1⅔ T
12	2 T
16	2⅔ T
20	3⅓ T
24	¼ cup
30	⅓ cup
40	⅜ cup
50	½ cup
60	⅔ cup

WEIGHT UNITS OF MEASURE

Solids are measured by weight. Solid foods include meat, produce, flour, and many other items. The traditional units of measure for weight in the United States are pounds and ounces. A weight ounce is typically a decimal, fraction, or a percent of a pound. *It is not the same, or equal to, a fluid ounce.* A fluid ounce is a volume unit of measure. A weight ounce is a solid unit of measure. The relationship between pounds and ounces is displayed in Table 7.3.

Accurate weight measurement is only achieved by using a scale. Different types of scales are available. A **baker's scale** is used in the baking and pastry professions. In commercial baking, flour must be weighted because of variations in compactness, grinding size, humidity, grain type, and other factors. The baker's scale measures flour, sugar, yeast, and other solid ingredients against a weight.

TABLE 7.3 U.S Weight Units of Measure and Their Equivalents

Pounds (lb, #)	Ounces (oz.)
1 pound	16 ounces
½ pound	8 ounces
¼ pound	4 ounces
⅛ pound	2 ounces

FIGURE 7.6

Baker's scale. Courtesy of the Edlund Co.
Photography by Thomas Myers

FIGURE 7.7

Portioning scale. Courtesy of the Edlund Co.
Photography by Thomas Myers

A portion-control scale is used to measure portion size. Meats, like a "quarter-pound" hamburger, are weighted prior to cooking to ensure the weight is ¼, or 25%, or 0.25, of a pound. Sliced deli meats are weighted before a sandwich is served to ensure the portion size is correct.

COUNT AS A UNIT OF MEASURE

Certain food products are individual units, and they are measured by **count**. Eggs, shrimp, apples, and bay leaves are examples of food products that might be measured by count. Count is not an exact measurement. Recipes that require total accuracy will measure count items, like eggs, by volume or weight. A recipe for egg bread will use a volume or a weight quantity for the eggs, rather than a count measure.

International Standard Units of Measure

THE METRIC SYSTEM

The **metric system** is the internationally recognized system for volume and weight measurement. It is a decimal-based system. It is used globally, except in the United States. However, the United States is slowly adapting to the metric system.

All food products produced and packaged in the United States display both the U.S. standard and the metric equivalent measurement on the package. All imported food products display the metric measurement on the package. Alcoholic beverages, except domestic beer, are packaged exclusively using metric volume units of measure.

It is common in U.S. kitchens to have U.S. standard and metric units of measure on volume measuring tools. It is also common to find metric units of measure on kitchen scales.

METRIC VOLUME UNITS OF MEASURE

The volume units of measure in the metric system are the liter (L) and milliliter (mL). One liter equals 1,000 milliliters. The relationship between the metric system and the U.S. standard system is shown in Table 7.4.

METRIC WEIGHT UNITS OF MEASURE

The weight units of measure in the metric system are kilogram (kg) and gram (g). A kilogram equals 1,000 grams. The relationship between the metric and U.S. standard system is shown in Table 7.5.

TABLE 7.4 Metric Volume Units of Measure and U.S. Equivalents*

Liter (L)	Milliliter (mL)	Fluid Ounces (Fl. oz.)	Gallon (G, gal.)	Quart (Qt.)	Pint (Pt.)	Cup (C, c)	Tablespoon (T, tbsp.)	Teaspoon (t, tsp.)
3.8 L	3,800 mL	128 fl. ounces	1 gallon	4 quarts	8 pints	16 cups		
1 L	1,000 mL	33.8 fl. ounces						
0.95 L	946 mL	32 fl. oz.	.25 gallon	1 quart	2 pints	4 cups		
	750 mL	25.4 fl. oz.						
	500 mL	16.9 fl. oz.						
0.47 L	474 mL	16 fl. oz.		.50 quart	1 pint	2 cups		
0.24 L	237 mL	8 fl. oz.		.25 quart	0.50 pint	1 cup		
	30 mL	1 fl. oz.						
	15 mL						1 T	
	5 mL							1 tsp.

*The conversion from liter/milliliter to gallon/quart/pint/cup/fluid ounce is a close approximation due to rounding.

TABLE 7.5 Metric Weight Units of Measure and U.S. Equivalents

Kilogram (kg)	Gram (g)	Pound (lb., #)	Ounce (oz.)
1 kilogram	1,000 grams	2.2 pounds	35.2 ounces
	454 grams	1 pound	16 ounces
	28.35 grams		1 ounce
	1 gram		0.035 ounces

Conversion between U.S. Units of Measure and the Metric System

Within the global community, it is common to purchase food products and alcoholic beverages that are sold in metric units of measure. It is also common to see recipes written in metric units of measure. However, in the United States, people are more comfortable with the U.S. standard units of measure. This situation has created a need to convert units of measure from the U.S. standard to metric, and from metric to the U.S. standard.

The conversion process is easy because the relationship between the differing units of measure is constant. **Constant** means it never changes. Therefore, a **multiplier**, or a number used to multiply by, represents the relationship between the U.S. standard units of measure and the metric system units of measure. These multipliers are decimal numbers. Multiplication with these decimal numbers results in the conversion between the U.S. standard and the metric system units of measure. Refer to Chapter 4 to review multiplication with decimals.

The conversion tables can be used to adjust a recipe's ingredients from U.S. standard units to metric units of measure, or from metric to U.S. standard units of measure. They can also be used to adjust the per-unit price of a recipe's ingredient. This is extremely useful with recipe and portion costing and menu pricing.

Table 7.6 displays the multipliers (decimal numbers) used to convert between the U. S. standard and the metric units of measure for volume. Table 7.7 displays the multipliers (decimal numbers) used to convert between the U.S. standard and the metric units of measure for weight. These conversion charts simplify the process for changing units of measure between the U.S. standard and the metric units. There are three steps for this process. Examples of these differing uses follow the conversion tables.

> **STEP 1:** Determine the unit of measure you have and find it on the table.
>
> **STEP 2:** Determine the unit of measure you need and find it on the table.
>
> **STEP 3:** Multiply the units of measure you have by the multiplier (decimal number) on the table to convert the units of measure.

TABLE 7.6 U.S.-to-Metric Conversion Volume Conversion Multipliers

To Change	To	Multiply By
Gallons	Liters	3.785
Liters	Quarts	1.0567
Quarts	Liters	.946
Pints	Liters	.474
Cups	Liters	.236
Fluid ounces	Milliliters	29.57
Tablespoons	Milliliters	14.79
Teaspoons	Milliliters	4.93

A recipe for cream of broccoli soup yields 2 gallons. The chef would like to know how many liters the recipe will yield.

> **CREAM OF BROCCOLI SOUP**
>
> The conversion is gallons to liters.
>
> **STEP 1:** The unit of measure for the soup is gallons.
>
> **STEP 2:** The new unit of measure for the soup is liters.
>
> **STEP 3:** The multiplier (decimal number) to change gallons to liters is 3.785 (see Table 7.6).
>
> 2 (gallons) × 3.785 = 7.57 liters
>
> Two gallons of cream of broccoli soup yields 7.57 liters.

 ## Weight Unit of Measure Conversion Table

Le French Cookbook lists the following ingredients for a pâté:

Ground beef 1 kilogram
Ground pork 500 grams
Ground veal 300 grams

You purchase meat by the pound. How many pounds of ground beef, ground pork, and ground veal should you order?

TABLE 7.7 U.S.-to-Metric Weight Conversion Multipliers

To Change	To	Multiply By
Kilograms	Pounds	2.2046
Pounds	Kilograms	0.4536
Grams	Pounds	0.0022
Pounds	Grams	453.5924
Grams	Weight ounces	0.0353
Weight ounces	Grams	28.3495

PÂTÉ

The conversion for ground beef is kilogram to pounds.

> **STEP 1:** **The recipe lists ground beef by the kilogram.**
>
> **STEP 2:** **You purchase ground beef by the pound.**
>
> **STEP 3:** **The multiplier (decimal number) to change kilograms to pounds is 2.2046 (see Table 7.7).**

1 kilogram (ground beef) × 2.2046 = 2.2046 pounds

2.2046 pounds × 16 ounces = 35.2736 ounces of ground beef, rounded to 35.3 ounces of ground beef

The conversion for ground pork is grams to pounds.

> **STEP 1:** **The recipe lists ground pork by the gram.**
>
> **STEP 2:** **You purchase ground pork by the pound.**
>
> **STEP 3:** **The multiplier (decimal number) to change grams to pounds is 0.0022 (see Table 7.7).**

500 grams (ground pork) × 0.0022 = 1.1 pounds

1.1 pounds × 16 ounces = 17.6 ounces of ground pork

The conversion for ground veal is grams to pounds.

> **STEP 1:** **The recipe lists ground veal by the gram.**
>
> **STEP 2:** **You purchase ground veal by the pound.**
>
> **STEP 3:** **The multiplier (decimal number) to change grams to pounds is 0.0022 (see Table 7.7).**

300 grams (ground veal) × 0.0022 = 0.66 pounds

0.66 pounds × 16 ounces = 10.56 ounces of ground veal, rounded to 10.6 ounces of ground veal

To prepare the pâté recipe, you should order the following:

Ground beef, 2.2 pounds, or 35.3 ounces

Ground pork, 1.1 pounds, or 17.6 ounces

Ground veal, 0.66 pounds, or 10.6 ounces

In the pâté example, the decimal product, or the answer, can be multiplied by 16, the number of ounces in a pound, to ensure the correct order quantity, converted from both kilograms and grams to pounds and ounces, is ordered.

Cost Conversions

Multipliers can also be used to convert cost per U.S. standard unit to cost per metric unit, or cost per metric unit to cost per U.S. standard unit.

OLIVE OIL

Olive oil is purchased in a 2-liter bottle for $4.50.

Our recipe uses 1 pint of olive oil.

How much does 1 pint of olive oil cost?

The cost per liter is as follows:

$4.50 (Cost for 2 liters / 2 (liters) = $2.25 per liter

Olive oil costs $2.25 per liter.

OLIVE OIL COST PER PINT

The conversion is liter to pint.

> **STEP 1:** **You need the cost per pint of olive oil.**
>
> **STEP 2:** **You have the cost per liter of olive oil.**
>
> **STEP 3:** **The multiplier (decimal number) to change pints to liters is 0.474. (Table 7.6).**

$2.25 (cost per liter) $\times$ 0.474 = $1.07

Olive oil costs $1.07 per pint.

The conversion multipliers provide a very useful tool to use both in the kitchen as you prepare foods and in the office as you cost recipes.

 Volume vs. Weight Controversy

Volume measurement is most accurate for liquids, while weight measurement is most accurate for solids. However, it is common to see recipes that do not follow the rules for accurate measurement.

Spices are often listed in recipes using a volume unit of measure. The quantities are too small to weigh, so they are measured by volume. Flour is often listed by the cup, tablespoon, or teaspoon, although it should be listed by weight. Dishers/scoops are volume-portioning tools that are often used to measure items that would be best measured by weight.

Whenever you encounter an item that is listed in the incorrect unit of measure, you should question the accuracy of the recipe. Some recipes will need to be adjusted so they will produce a consistent product every time they are prepared. Appendix II provides a list of a variety of common food items by volume and weight to assist with the adjustment of recipes that list ingredients in the incorrect units of measure.

 ## Conclusion

Understanding units of measure is an important cornerstone to achieving a successful career in the foodservice industry. It is critical that you can identify different units of measure and that you understand their relationships to one another. This knowledge will help you with food and beverage purchasing, recipe preparation, product consistency, recipe costing, menu pricing, and profitability. You should review this chapter often during your career in the foodservice industry.

 ## Units of Measure: REVIEW PROBLEMS

1. How many fluid ounces are in the following volume units of measure?

a. 1 gallon

b. ½ gallon

c. 1 quart

d. 1 pint

e. 1 cup

f. 1 liter

g. 750 mL

h. 500 mL

i. 250 mL

2. How many quarts are in 1 gallon?

3. What percent of a gallon is 1 quart?

   a. What is the fraction equivalent?

   b. What is the decimal equivalent?

4. How many pints are in 1 quart?

5. What percent of a quart is 1 pint?

   a. What is the fraction equivalent?

   b. What is the decimal equivalent?

6. How many teaspoons are in 1 tablespoon?

7. How many weight ounces are in 1 pound?

8. What is the difference between a fluid ounce and a weight ounce?

9. How many grams are in 1 kilogram?

10. How many grams are in a pound?

11. What is a multiplier?

12. Why can a multiplier be used to convert between the U.S. standard and the metric system units of measure?

Use the three steps for unit of measure conversions and Tables 7.6 and 7.7 to answer the following problems.

STEP 1: Determine the unit of measure you have, and find it on the table.

STEP 2: Determine the unit of measure you need, and find it on the table.

STEP 3: Multiply the units of measure you have by the decimal multiplier in the table to convert the units of measure.

13. *Le French Cookbook* lists the amount of whipping cream needed for a recipe as 500 mL. You purchase 1 quart of whipping cream for $2.39.

   a. How many milliliters (mL) are in 1 quart?

   b. Do you have enough whipping cream?

   c. What is the cost per mL for the whipping cream?

   d. What is the total cost for 500 mL of whipping cream?

14. *Le French Cookbook* lists the amount of meat needed as 1.5 kilograms. You purchase 5 pounds of meat at $2.25 per pound.

   a. What is the multiplier for changing kilograms to pounds?

   b. How many pounds equal 1.5 kilograms?

   c. Do you have enough meat for the recipe?

   d. How many pounds of meat will be left after the recipe is prepared?

   e. What is the total cost of the meat in the recipe?

15. A 750-mL bottle of white wine costs $10.00. Your wine glasses hold 5 fluid ounces.

   a. How many fluid ounces are in 750 mL?

   b. How many mL are in 1 fluid ounce?

   c. How many glasses of wine can you serve from a 750-mL bottle?

   d. What is the cost per serving for this wine?

16. Convert the following recipe from U.S. standard units to metric units.

Ingredient	U.S. Units	Metric Units
Chicken stock	½ gallon	
Chicken	1 pound	
Carrots	¼ pound	
Potatoes	¾ pound	

Running Case Study

Step III

The units of measure that are used in professional kitchens, and in standardized recipes, have been discussed in this chapter. Thomas Morgan must now review the three standardized recipes he wrote at the end of Chapter 6. All of his standardized recipe ingredients need to be placed in the correct U.S. standard units of measure. The tables in this chapter and Appendix II can be used for this task. Appendix II is used to convert an item to its correct unit of measure: volume to weight or weight to volume.

Thomas will use the ingredient quantities that prepare 50 portions. He will look at the ingredient list and convert the units of measure to the correct measurements. After the conversion is complete, Thomas will need to test these recipes to ensure the taste and number of portions are correct. Based on the results of his testing, some adjustments may have to be made to the ingredient quantities for the real world.

Standardized Recipe #1

The Best Meatballs Ever

Preparation and Cooking Time: 1.5 hours **Recipe Yield: 60 each**
Portion Size: 2 each **Number of Portions: 30**

Quantity	Ingredients	Preparation Method
5 pounds	Ground beef	
5 pounds	Ground pork	
10 cups	Italian bread crumbs	
10 each	Eggs	
	Recipe served 30 portions.	
	To serve 50 portions:	
	New/Old = Conversion factor	
	50/30 = 1.67	
5 pounds × 1.67 = 8.3 pounds	Ground beef	
5 pounds × 1.67 = 8.3 pounds	Ground pork	
10 cups × 1.67 = 16.7 cups	Italian bread crumbs	
10 eggs × 1.67 = 16.7	Eggs	
	Correct Units of Measure	
8.3 pounds (weight)	Ground beef	
8.3 pounds (weight)	Ground pork	
3.13 pounds (weight, not volume)	Italian bread crumbs	
17 each (count); rounded from 16.7 to 17	Eggs	

Bread crumbs should be measured by weight, not volume.

Appendix II lists 1 cup bread crumbs = 3 weight ounces.

or

1 pound bread crumbs = 5.34 cups

This recipe lists 16.7 cups.

16.7 cups 3 ounces = 50.1 ounces

50.1 ounces ÷ 16 (ounces per pound) = 3.13 pounds

or

16.7 cups ÷ 5.34 cups (one pound) = 3.13 pounds

Standardized Recipe #2

Beef Braised in Red Wine Sauce

Preparation and Cooking Time: 3.5 hours
Portion Size:

Recipe Yield:
Number of Portions: 6

Quantity	Ingredients	Preparation Method
2 T	Vegetable oil	
4 pound	Beef roast	
1 T	Butter	
3 T	Yellow onion, chopped	
2 T	Carrot, chopped	
2 T	Celery, chopped	
1.5 cups	Dry red wine	
1 cup	Beef stock	
1.5 T	Italian tomatoes	
Pinch	Thyme	
1/8 tsp.	Marjoram	
	Recipe served 6 portions.	
	To serve 50 portions:	
	New/Old = Conversion factor	
	50/6 = 8.3	
2 T × 8.3 = 16.67 T	Vegetable oil	
4 pounds × 8.3 = 33.2 pounds	Beef roast	
1 T × 8.3 = 8.3 T	Butter	
3 T × 8.3 = 24.9 T	Yellow onion, chopped	
2 T × 8.3 = 16.6 T	Carrot, chopped	
2 T × 8.3 = 16.6 T	Celery, chopped	
1.5 cups × 8.3 = 12.45 cups	Dry red wine	
1 cup × 8.3 = 8.3 cups	Beef stock	
1.5 T × 8.3 = 12.45 T	Italian tomatoes	
Pinch × 8.3 = ?	Thyme	
1/8 tsp × 8.3 = 1 tsp.	Marjoram	
	Correct Units of Measure	
1 cup, 2 tsp. (volume)	Vegetable oil	
33.2 pounds (weight)	Beef roast	
4 ounces (weight)	Butter	
12 ounces (weight)	Yellow onion, chopped	
4 ounces (weight)	Carrot, chopped	
4 ounces (weight)	Celery, chopped	
3 quarts, 1/2 cup (volume)	Dry red wine	
2 quarts, 3 fl. oz. (volume)	Beef stock	
6 ounces (weight)	Italian tomatoes	
1/2 tsp. (volume)	Pinch	
1 tsp. (volume)	Marjoram	

Vegetable oil is a liquid and measured by volume.

16 T = 1 cup, 1 T = 3 tsp.

The recipe uses 16.67 T = 1 cup, 2 tsp.

Butter is measured by weight, or melted and measured by volume.

From Appendix II: 2 T = 1 ounce

Recipe uses 8 T = 4 ounces, .3 T = 1 tsp.

Converted to 4 ounces (weight, rounded)

Onions are measured by weight.

From Appendix II: 1 cup = 8 ounces

Recipe uses 24.9 T = 1.5 cups plus 1 T (volume)

Converted to 12 ounces (weight, rounded)

Carrots and celery are measured by weight.

Appendix II: 1 cup = 4 ounces

Recipe uses 16.6 T = 1 cup, 2 tsp.

Converted to 4 ounces (weight, rounded)

Dry red wine is measured by volume.

Recipe uses 12.45 cups = 3 quarts, .5 cups (volume, rounded)

Beef stock is measured by volume.

Recipe uses 8.3 cups = 2 quarts, 3 fl. oz. (volume)

Italian tomatoes are measured by volume.

Recipe uses 12.34 T = 0.75 cup = 6 fl. oz. (volume, rounded)

Thyme is measured by volume.

Recipe uses a pinch × 8.3.

Converted to 0.5 or ½ tsp. (volume, rounded)

Marjoram is measured by volume.

Recipe uses 1 tsp.

Standardized Recipe #3

Veal Scaloppine with Lemon Sauce

Preparation and Cooking Time: 5 min.
Portion Size: 0.25 pound

Recipe Yield:
Number of Portions: 4

Quantity	Ingredients	Preparation Methods
2 T	Vetetable oil	
1/4 cup	Butter	
1 pound	Veal, pounded flat	
3/4 cup	Flour	
2 T	Lemon juice	
2 T	Parsley, chopped	
1/2	Lemon, sliced	
	Recipe served 4 portions.	
	To serve 50 portions:	
	New/Old = Conversion factor	
	50/4 = 12.5	
2 T × 12.5 = 25 T	Vegetable oil	
1/4 cup × 12.5 = 3.125 cups	Butter	
1 pound × 12.5 = 12.5 pounds	Veal, pounded flat	
3/4 cup × 12.5 = 9.375 cups	Flour	
2 T × 12.5 = 25 T	Lemon juice	
2 T × 12.5 = 25 T	Parsley, chopped	
1/2 × 12.5 = 6.25	Lemon, sliced	
	Correct Units of Measure	
1½ cups plus 1 T (volume)	Vegetable oil	
1½ pounds (weight)	Butter	
12.5 pounds (weight)	Veal, pounded flat	
2.34 pounds (weight)	Flour	
1½ cups plus 1 T (volume)	Lemon juice	
1½ cups plus 1 T (volume)	Parsley, chopped	
6¼ each (count)	Lemon, sliced	

Using the tables in this chapter and Appendix II, explain the process Thomas used to arrive at his ingredient quantities for veal scaloppine with lemon sauce.

Then convert your measurements listed in the three recipes you have chosen to the correct units of measure.

CHAPTER **8**

Foodservice-Specific Terminology *and* Mathematics

Part I
As Purchased, Edible Portion, As Served, and Yield Percent

"The foodservice industry has its own unique terminology. The professional uses it daily."

—Terri Jones

Food products are unique. One of the most unique features is that the product is purchased in a form that is very different than the way it is eventually served to the guest. This uniqueness gives the foodservice industry its own terminology to describe the different states of the food products, from purchasing to service.

LEARNING OBJECTIVES

1. To fully comprehend the following terms:
   a. As purchased or AP
   b. Edible portion or EP
   c. As served or AS
   d. Yield percent

As Purchased, Edible Portion, As Served

A basic understanding of the terms **as purchased (AP)**, **edible portion (EP)**, and **as served (AS)** will impact your success with foodservice mathematics more than any other factor that comes to mind. The amount of a foodservice operation's profitability hinges on your understanding of these three terms.

These terms will be explained using a National Association of Meat Purveyors (NAMP) 109 prime rib roast as an example. The prime rib roast is purchased, roasted, and prepared to be served.

FIGURE 8.1

Prime rib roast, total edible portion (EP) and as served (AS) portion.

Photography by Thomas Myers

AS PURCHASED

> ### AS PURCHASED
>
> This is the product as it is purchased.
>
> The item has an as purchased, or AP, unit of measure.
>
> The item has an as purchased, or AP, price, and price per unit of measure.

> ### AP EXAMPLE
>
> You purchase a NAMP 109 prime rib roast.
>
> The roast weighs 20 pounds.
>
> The AP unit of measure is pounds.
>
> The AP weight is 20 pounds.
>
> The roast costs $60.00.
>
> $60.00 (cost for roast) ÷ 20 (pounds) = $3.00 (cost per pound)
>
> The cost per pound is $3.00.
>
> The AP price is $60.00.
>
> The AP price per pound is $3.00.

EDIBLE PORTION

> ### EDIBLE PORTION
>
> This is the edible portion, or EP, the amount of product available to serve the guest after cleaning, trimming, and cooking the product.
>
> The item will have an edible portion, or EP, unit of measure.
>
> The item will have an edible portion, or EP, price per unit of measure.

The NAMP 109 prime rib roast will have an EP weight less than (<) the AP weight, due to trimming and shrinkage during roasting.

The NAMP 109 prime rib roast will have an EP price per pound greater than (>) the AP price per pound due to trimming and shrinkage during roasting.

AS SERVED

> ### AS SERVED
>
> This is the product as it is served to the guest.
>
> The item has an as served, or AS, unit of measure.
>
> The item has an as served, or AS, price per unit of measure.
>
> As served is discussed in detail in Chapter 11, "Menu Pricing."

The NAMP 109 prime rib roast is AS to the guest by the weight ounce or (possibly) pound.

The NAMP 109 prime rib roast has an AS price by the weight ounce or (possibly) pound.

 **Yield Percent**

The majority of food purchased is trimmed and/or cooked. This process causes the EP weight to vary from the AP weight. A food item can shrink, resulting in a loss of AP weight, or the item can expand, resulting in a gain over the AP weight.

The difference between the AP weight (volume) and the EP weight (volume) is called a **yield percent**.

YIELD PERCENT FORMULAS

To determine a product's yield:

$$\text{Yield percent} = \frac{\text{EP weight (or volume)}}{\text{AP weight (or volume)}}$$

To determine the correct amount of product to order:

$$\text{AP quantity} = \frac{\text{EP weight (or volume)}}{\text{Yield percent}}$$

To determine the actual cost of the food served to the guest:

$$\text{EP or AS price} = \frac{\text{AP price per unit}}{\text{Yield percent}}$$

NAMP 109 PRIME RIB ROAST EXAMPLE OF YIELD PERCENTAGE

The NAMP 109 prime rib roast with an AP weight of 20 pounds is trimmed.

Trimming causes a "loss" of AP weight.

The NAMP 109 prime rib roast is roasted.

Roasting causes a "loss" of AP weight.

The NAMP 109 prime rib roast is weighed after roasting.

It weighs 10 pounds.

This is the EP weight.

WHAT IS THE YIELD PERCENT?

The formula for yield percent is as follows:

$$\text{Yield percent} = \frac{\text{EP weight}}{\text{AP weight}}$$

The yield percent for the NAMP 109 prime rib roast is as follows:

$$\text{Yield percent} = \frac{10 \text{ pounds}}{20 \text{ pounds}} = 50\%$$

The yield percent is also equal to ½, or 0.50.

WHAT DOES A YIELD PERCENT MEAN?

A yield percent of 50% means one-half (½, 0.5, or 50%) of the roast is lost in the trimming and cooking process. There are only 10 pounds of product available (edible portion) to serve your guests from a 20-pound AP roast.

DOES A YIELD PERCENT IMPACT FOOD PURCHASING?

The yield percent of a food product has a direct impact on the quantity of product purchased. The amount of product purchased is not equal to the amount of product available to serve the guest.

$$\text{AP weight} \neq \text{EP weight}$$

NAMP 109 PRIME RIB ROAST EXAMPLE FOR PURCHASING

40 guests are invited to dinner.
>   The menu includes an 8-ounce portion of prime rib.
>   How many pounds of NAMP 109 prime rib roast should be purchased?

40 (guests) × 8 (ounces) = 320 (ounces)

There are 16 ounces in 1 pound.

320 (ounces) ÷ 16 (ounces per pound) = 20 pounds

You need 20 pounds of roast to serve 40 guests.

Is that 20 pounds AP or 20 pounds EP?

It is 20 pounds EP.

How many pounds of NAMP 109 should be purchased?

$$\text{AP quantity} = \frac{\text{EP weight}}{\text{Yield percent}}$$

$$\text{AP quantity} = \frac{20 \text{ (pounds EP)}}{50 \text{ \%, or } 0.5 \text{ (yield percent)}}$$

AP quantity = 40 pounds NAMP 109 prime rib roast

Forty (40) pounds of NAMP 109 prime rib roast should be purchased to serve each of the 40 guests an 8-ounce portion.

DOES THE YIELD PERCENT HAVE AN IMPACT ON FOOD COST?

The yield percent of a food product also has a **significant impact on** food cost. The increase in amount of food purchased directly impacts the cost of food served to the guest.

NAMP 109 PRIME RIB ROAST EXAMPLE FOR FOOD COST

The roast's AP cost is $3.00 per pound.

> To purchase 40 pounds AP, it costs the following:
>
> $3.00 (cost per pound) × 40 (pounds) = $120.00 (cost for 40 pounds)
>
> $120.00 (AP cost for 40 pounds) ÷ 20 (EP yield) = $6.00 per pound

---

YIELD PERCENT FOOD COST FORMULA

$$EP = \frac{AP \text{ price per unit}}{\text{Yield percent}}$$

$$EP \text{ price} = \frac{\$3.00 \text{ (price for pound AP)}}{50\%, \text{ or } 0.5}$$

$$EP = \$6.00 \text{ per pound}$$

The actual cost per pound to serve the guest is $6.00 per pound.

The yield percent is used to determine the amount of food to purchase and to determine the actual cost to serve the food to a guest. These calculations are critical to the success of a foodservice operation.

 **Conclusion**

The terminology and mathematics covered in this chapter are the most important tools to understand and use to help you to run a profitable foodservice operation. Understanding the difference between the AP unit of measure and cost and the EP and/or AS unit of measure and cost is crucial for an operation to be profitable and successful. This information is challenging, but practicing these calculations will help you to fully understand this material.

Foodservice-Specific Mathematics: Part I REVIEW PROBLEMS

1. Define the term "as purchased."

2. Define the term "edible portion."

3. Define the term "as served."

4. In the table that follows, fill in the Yield Percent column, using the following formula:

$$\text{Yield percent} = \frac{\text{EP weight}}{\text{AP weight}}$$

Item Number	As Purchased	Edible Portion	Yield Percent
1	7 pounds	3.5 pounds	
2	5 pounds	2 pounds	
3	10 pounds	6 pounds	
4	1 kilogram	500 grams	
5	1 gallon	64 fl. oz.	
6	1 quart	8 fl. oz.	
7	1 liter	750 mL	
8	4 liters	1 liter	
9	50 pounds	12.5 pounds	
10	40 pounds	15 pounds	

In the table that follows, fill in the AP Quantity column, using the following formula:

$$\text{AP quantity} = \frac{\text{EP/AS quantity}}{\text{Yield percent}}$$

Item Number	EP/AS Quantity	Yield Percent	AP Quantity
11	6 ounces	50%	
12	1 gallon	30%	
13	15 pounds	40%	
14	11 pounds	65%	
15	8 pounds	25%	
16	2 kilograms	75%	
17	750 mL	50%	
18	64 fl. oz.	10%	
19	1 quart	25%	
20	15 pounds	15%	

In the table that follows, fill in the EP/AS Price column, using the following formula:

$$\text{EP/AS Price} = \frac{\text{AP price}}{\text{Yield percent}}$$

Item Number	AP Price	Yield Percent	EP/AS Price
21	$2.25	25%	
22	$3.25	70%	
23	$0.69	100%	
24	$5.00	50%	
25	$1.75	35%	
26	$0.50	33%	
27	$10.00	90%	
28	$1.00	10%	
29	$4.50	45%	
30	$2.50	75%	

Foodservice-Specific Terminology *and* Mathematics

Part II
The Impact of As Purchased and Edible Portion on the Major Food Groups

"Quantities change as the food is prepared for service. Sometimes the food shrinks, while other times the food expands."

—TERRI JONES

Each food product groups has a unique relationship between its as purchased (AP) and edible portion (EP) yields. This uniqueness is caused by the variety of ways different products are purchased, cleaned, trimmed, cooked, and ultimately served. Knowledge of the changes in food quantity as the item goes from its AP state to its EP state has a great impact on a restaurant's ability to make a profit.

Remember that the AP price of a food product, adjusted by the yield percent, equals the EP cost for every menu item. The EP cost is the cost of the food that is served to the guest.

LEARNING OBJECTIVES

1. To gain knowledge of the major food groups
2. To understand the relationship between AP quantity and cost and EP quantity and cost for the major food groups
3. To understand the process and importance of a yield test for meats
4. To distinguish between EP and AS

Food Purchasing

All of the food served in a restaurant has an AP quantity and cost. The relationship between the AP quantity and cost and the EP quantity and cost will vary based on the food's product group. This variation impacts the actual cost to serve the meal to the guest.

Food Product Groups

MEATS

Meats include beef, veal/calf, pork, and lamb. Meat is AP by the pound, both for weight and cost. Meat can be AP in many different forms. It can be purchased as a whole carcass, a side of beef, a quarter of a side, an oven-ready roast or as a portion-controlled hamburger patty.

> If meat is purchased in a portion-controlled unit:
>
> AP weight > EP weight (due to shrinkage in cooking)
>
> AP cost per portion = EP cost per portion
>
> **Portion-Control Example**
> You purchase a 20-pound box of 8-ounce rib eye steaks.
> The AP price per pound is $5.00.
> An 8-ounce steak is ½ (or 0.5 or 50%) of 1 pound (16 ounces).
> The AP price per rib eye steak is $2.50.
> The EP cost to serve each steak is $2.50.
>
> AP cost per portion (steak) = EP cost per portion (steak)
> The EP steak will weigh less than (<) 8 ounces after the cooking process.
> If meat is purchased in a non-portion-controlled form, then
> AP weight will be greater than (>) EP weight (due to trimming and shrinkage during cooking)
> AP cost per pound < EP cost per pound

Non-Portion-Controlled Example

You purchase an 8-pound pork shoulder.

The AP price per pound is $3.50

The EP weight after cooking is 6.5 pounds.

$$\text{The yield percent} = \frac{\text{EP weight}}{\text{AP weight}}$$

$$\text{Yield \%} = \frac{6.5 \text{ pounds}}{8 \text{ pounds}} = .8125 \text{ or } 81.25\%$$

The EP cost per pound is

$$\text{EP cost per pound} = \frac{\text{AP price per pound}}{\text{Yield percent}}$$

$$\text{EP cost per pound} = \frac{\$3.50}{.8125} = \$4.3077, \text{ rounded to } \$4.31 \text{ per pound}$$

AP weight > EP weight

AP price per pound < EP price per pound

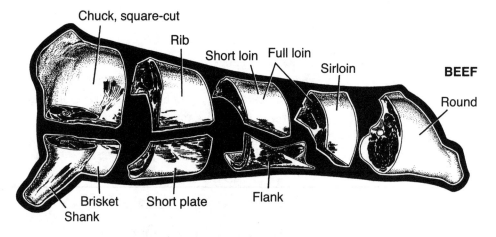

FIGURE 9.1

Beef cuts. Courtesy of National Live Stock and Meat Board.
Copyright Cattlemen's Beef Board & National Cattlemen's Beef Association

POULTRY

Poultry includes chicken, turkey, duck, goose, and game birds. Poultry is similar to meats in terms of its AP and EP relationships. Poultry can be purchased in portion-controlled units, such as boneless skinless chicken breasts. The breasts are sold by the pound, and each breast or portion has a certain weight in ounces. There is a loss of AP weight during cooking, but the AP and EP cost per portion are equal.

FIGURE 9.2

Chicken, whole and quartered.

Photography by Thomas Myers

Poultry can also be AP as a whole bird, by the pound, for weight and cost. Once roasted, it will have a loss of AP weight, and therefore, an increase in EP cost per pound.

SHELLFISH

Shellfish are animals that live in shells under water. They include both crustaceans and mollusks. The AP cost for shellfish is by the piece or by a certain number per pound, bushel, or gallon. Therefore, shellfish are considered a portion-controlled item. The AP cost per portion is equal to the EP cost per portion.

FINFISH

Finfish are animals that live in fresh or salt water. They can be flat or round. Finfish can be AP in many different market forms. These forms can include both portion-controlled units and units that will have a yield variance between their AP and EP weight and cost.

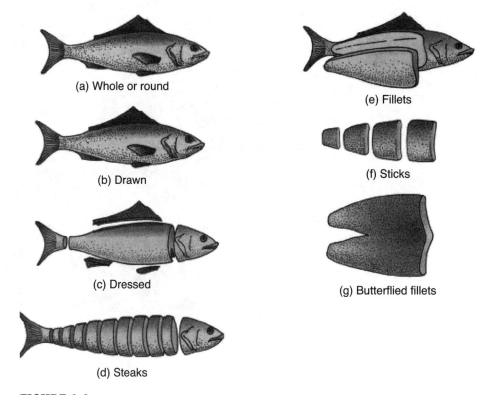

FIGURE 9.3

The market forms of fish: (a) whole or round fish; (b) drawn; (c) dressed; (d) steaks; (e) fillets; (f) sticks; (g) butterflied fillets.

Courtesy Professional Cooking, Fifth Edition, by Wayne Gisslen, 2003: John Wiley & Sons, Inc. p. 361

 # Yield Test for Non-Portioned-Controlled Meats, Poultry, and Finfish

Meats, poultry, and/or finfish items that are AP in any form other than a portion-controlled unit are cleaned and trimmed before the cooking process begins. The process of cleaning and trimming produces a **fabricated**, or recipe-ready, item. This process also produces by-products that can have value, both in terms of product and money, to the foodservice operation.

YIELD TEST EXAMPLE
AP rib primal
AP weight = 26 pounds
AP price = $1.89 per pound
Total cost for rib primal
26 (pounds) × $1.89 (price per pound) = $49.14

The rib primal is trimmed into 5 fabricated components that total 26 AP pounds

15-pound oven-ready rib roast

3.5 pounds stew beef

2.5 pounds short ribs

2.5 pounds beef bones

2.5 pounds fat

The yield on the rib roast *fabricated* from the rib primal

$$\text{Yield percent} = \frac{\text{EP weight}}{\text{AP weight}}$$

$$\text{Yield percent} = \frac{15 \text{ (pounds)}}{26 \text{ (pounds)}} = .5769 \text{ or } 57.69\%$$

The By-Products

Fabricating a rib roast from a rib primal has a 57.69% yield.

100% − 57.69% = 42.31%

The by-products have a 42.31% yield.

BY-PRODUCTS MARKET VALUE EXAMPLE

Oven-ready rib roast's "market value" is $2.89 per pound

Stew beef's "market value" is $2.39 per pound

Short ribs' "market value" is $1.79 per pound

Beef bones' "market value" is $0.50 per pound

Beef fat's "market value" is $0.05 per pound

The Value of the By-Products

Stew Beef

3.5 (pounds stew beef) × $2.39 (price per pound) = $8.365 rounded to $8.37

Short Ribs

2.5 (pounds of short ribs) × $1.79 (price per pound) = $4.475 rounded to $4.48

Beef Bones

2.5 (pounds of beef bones) × $0.50 (price per pound) = $1.25

Beef Fat

2.5 (pounds of beef fat) × $0.05 (price per pound) = $0.125 rounded to $0.13

The Total Value of the By-Products

$8.37 (stew beef) + $4.48 (short ribs) + $1.25 (beef bones) + $0.13 (beef fat) = $14.23

AP COST OF THE RIB ROAST FABRICATED FROM RIB PRIMAL

AP cost of the rib primal = $49.14

AP cost of the by-products (based on market value) = $14.23

AP cost of the fabricated rib roast =

AP cost of the rib primal − AP cost of the by-product's market value

AP cost of the fabricated rib roast = $49.14 − $14.13

AP cost of the fabricated rib roast = $35.01

AP price per pound for fabricated rib roast =

Cost of rib roast ÷ Number of pounds

AP price per pound for the *fabricated* rib roast =

$35.01 (cost of roast) ÷ 15 (pounds) = $2.334

$2.334, rounded to $2.33 cost per pound

The cost of the fabricated rib roast, at $2.33 per pound, is compared to the cost of an AP rib roast oven ready.

AP EQUIVALENT COST OF OVEN-READY RIB ROAST

AP market value of oven-ready rib roast = $2.89 per pound

AP price for equivalent 15-pound oven-ready rib roast is

15 (pounds) × $2.89 (oven-ready price per pound) = $43.35

$43.35 (AP price 15-pound oven-ready roast) − $35.01 (AP price fabricated roast) = $8.34

The equivalent rib roast purchased oven ready is $8.34 > the fabricated rib roast.

The cost of the fabricated rib roast is less than (<) the cost of a rib roast oven ready.

Conclusions of a Yield Test

A yield test produces valuable information about the actual AP cost of meat and poultry products that are fabricated within the foodservice operation. The yield test example above details the actual AP cost per pound of the rib roast fabricated from a rib primal. The actual cost per pound can be compared to the AP cost per pound for a rib roast that is purchased oven ready.

AP cost for rib roast from the rib primal is $2.33 per pound.

AP cost for an oven-ready rib roast is $2.89 per pound.

AP price savings per pound

> $2.89 (AP price oven-ready rib roast) − $2.33 (AP price fabricated rib roast) = $0.56
>
> The AP cost per pound for the *fabricated* rib roast is $0.56 less than (<) the oven-ready rib roast.

This cost comparison shows that the fabricated rib roast from the rib primal cost per pound is less than (<) the oven-ready rib roast.

The actual cost per pound for the rib roast is the major factor to consider when deciding which form of product to purchase; the rib primal or the oven-ready rib roast. Other factors to consider are the culinary staff's expertise in product fabrication and how the by-products might be used. If the culinary staff can fabricate the product, and the by-products can be used in other menu items, then price is the only consideration. If your staff cannot fabricate the product and/or you cannot use the by-products, then the oven-ready roast might be the best product to purchase.

Produce

Produce includes both fruits and vegetables, and is purchased by every foodservice operation. Produce is available in four market forms: fresh, frozen, canned, and dehydrated.

FRESH PRODUCE

Fresh produce can be served AP. This means the yield is 100%.

> Fresh berries are often served AP.*
>
> AP weight = EP weight
>
> AP price = EP price
>
> *If some of the fresh berries are unusable, the yield will be less than (<) 100%.

Fresh produce can also be trimmed and cooked before it is served. This means the yield is < 100%.

> Broccoli florets are often trimmed and cooked before serving.
>
> AP weight > EP weight
>
> AP price per pound < EP price per pound

FROZEN PRODUCE

Produce is cleaned and trimmed before freezing. This means the yield on frozen produce is 100%.

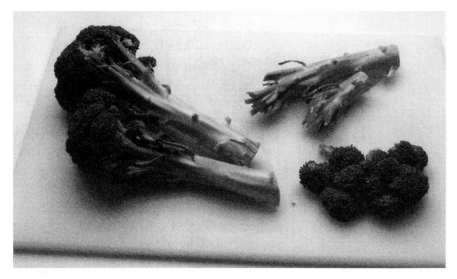

FIGURE 9.4

Broccoli whole to flowerettes and stems.

Photography by Thomas Myers

A 5-pound bag of frozen peas weighs 5 pounds after heating.

AP weight = EP weight

AP price = EP price

Frozen orange juice is AP as a concentrate and is reconstituted before it can be served. Reconstitution is the process of adding water, or volume, to the AP orange juice concentrate. This means the yield increases and is greater than (>) 100%.

FROZEN ORANGE JUICE CONCENTRATE EXAMPLE

AP 16-fl. oz. can of frozen orange juice

Three 16-fl.-oz. cans of water are added to the 16 fl. oz. of orange juice concentrate

16 fl. oz. orange juice + 16 fl. oz. water + 16 fl. oz. water + 16 fl. oz. water = 64 fl. oz. of ready-to-serve orange juice

AP volume = 16 fluid ounces

EP volume = 64 fluid ounces

$$\text{Yield percent} = \frac{\text{EP volume}}{\text{AP volume}}$$

$$\text{Yield percent} = \frac{64 \text{ fl. oz.}}{16 \text{ fl. oz.}}$$

Yield percent = 4.00, or 400%

AP volume < EP volume

AP frozen orange juice concentrate price = $1.60

AP volume = 16 fl. oz.

AP price per fl. oz. = $1.60 (price per can) ÷ 16 (fl. oz. per can) = $0.10 per fl. oz.

AP price per fl. oz. = .10

EP cost per fl. oz. =

$$\frac{\text{AP price per fl. oz.} = .10 \text{ (price per fl. oz.)}}{\text{Yield percent} = 4.00 \text{ or } 400\%}$$

EP cost per fl. oz. = $0.025 rounded to .03.

AP per fl. oz. is greater than (>) EP price per fl. oz.

For any frozen product that is reconstituted before serving, the yield percent is greater than (>) 100% and the EP cost per unit is less than (<) the AP cost per unit.

CANNED PRODUCE

The canning process places cleaned and trimmed produce into a can with water. The addition of water adds weight and/or volume to the can. When the can is opened, the water is drained. This yields the drained weight/volume for canned produce.

AS PURCHASED (AP) CANNED PRODUCE

AP weight/volume > EP weight/volume (drained weight/volume)

AP price per unit < EP per unit (drained weight/volume)

The exception to this is recipe-ready canned tomatoes. Tomatoes are canned in many forms, from whole peeled to paste. When canned tomatoes are used in a recipe, the entire can's contents are placed into the recipe. This includes any water that was added in the canning process.

CANNED TOMATOES

AP weight/volume = EP weight/volume

AP price = EP price

TABLE 9.1 Common Can and Jar Sizes (Average Net Weight or Fluid Measure and Average Volume per Can)

Can Size	Average Net Weight or Fluid Measurement per Can		Average Volume per Can	
	Customary	Metric	Cups	Liters
No. 10	6 lb (96 oz.) to 7 lb 5 oz. (117 oz.)	2.72 kg to 3.31 kg	12 cups to 13-2/3 cups	2.84 L to 3.24 L
No. 3 Cyl	51 oz. (3 lb 3 oz.) or 46 fl oz. (1 qt 14 fl. oz.)	1.44 kg or 1.36 L	5-3/4 cups	1.36 L
No. 2-1/2	26 oz. (1 lb to 10 oz.) to 30 oz. (1 lb to 14 oz.)	737 g to 850 g	3-1/2 cups	0.83 L
No. 2 Cyl	24 fl oz.	709 mL	3 cups	0.71 L
No. 2	20 oz. (1 lb 4 oz.) or 18 fl. oz. (1 lb 2 fl. oz.)	567 g or 532 mL	2-1/2 cups	0.59 L
No. 303 (old)	16 oz. (1 lb) to 18 fl. oz. (1 lb 1 oz.)	453 g to 481 g	2 cups	0.47 L
No. 300 (new)	14 oz. to 16 oz. (1 lb)	396 g to 453 g	1-3/4 cups	0.41 L
No. 2 (Vacuum)	12 oz.	340 g	1-1/2 cups	0.36 L
No. 1 (Picnic)	10-1/2 oz. to 12 oz.	297 g to 340 g	1-1/4 cups	0.30 L
8 oz.	8 oz.	226 g	1 cup	0.24L

USDA Food and Nutrition Service, *Food Buying Guide for Child Nutrition Programs*, revised November 2001, p. 1–30, www.fns.usda.gov/tn/Resources/fbguide_Introduction.pdf.

DEHYDRATED PRODUCE

Produce is dehydrated by the removal of water. Dried fruit is commonly used in its dehydrated state. This means the yield is 100%.

DRIED FRUIT

AP weight = EP weight

AP price per unit = EP price per unit

Dried vegetables are reconstituted before/during cooking by the addition of water and/or stock. This process adds weight/volume to the dried vegetables and increases the yield to greater than (>) 100%.

DRIED VEGETABLES

AP weight < EP weight

AP price > EP price

Dairy Products

Butter, hard and soft cheese, cream, half and half, milk, frozen desserts, and margarine are dairy products. Dairy products are used in their AP state both for immediate consumption and in a recipe. The yield is 100%.

DAIRY PRODUCTS

AP volume/weight = EP volume/weight

AP cost = EP cost

Pasta, Rice, and Legumes

Pasta is unleavened dough made by combining flour with water and/or eggs. Rice is an edible seed from a semiaquatic grass. Legumes are the edible seeds of plants that produce a single row of seeds inside a pod. Some pods are edible as well.

Pasta, rice, and legumes share a common method of preparation. They are prepared by boiling or simmering in a liquid. As they cook, they absorb moisture. This increases the weight or volume of these products. Therefore, the yield is greater than (>) 100%.

PASTA, RICE, AND LEGUMES

AP weight < EP weight (AP by weight, often EP by volume)

AP cost > EP cost

Miscellaneous Items

The majority of miscellaneous items are ingredients added to recipes. The AP quantity unit of measure is often different than the recipe unit of measure. The units of measure need to be converted to accurately measure ingredients and to calculate the EP cost. Some miscellaneous items are costly; others are not.

FAT AND OILS

Fat is an animal product and is solid at room temperature. Oil is from plants and is liquid at room temperature. Fat and oil are AP by weight or volume, but are EP in volume units of measure. For example, butter is solid at room temperature, AP by weight but measured by volume units. The yield on fat and oil is 100%.

FAT AND OILS

AP volume = EP volume

AP price = EP price

FLOUR AND SUGAR

Flour and sugar are used in many recipes. Some recipe quantities are small and are measured by volume. Flour and sugar used in baking and pastry is measured by weight. The yield on flour and sugar is 100%.

FLOUR AND SUGAR

AP weight = Recipe ingredient weight

AP cost per pound = Recipe ingredient weight per pound

HERBS, SPICES, AND SEASONINGS

Herbs, spices, and seasonings are used in small quantities in recipes to develop unique tastes and flavors. They are AP fresh, dried, or liquid. Often they are sold by the bunch, by the weight ounce, or by volume, but they are portioned by volume units of measure.

The use of small quantities and the difference between the AP unit of measure and the recipe ingredient unit of measure make costing these items tedious. It can be done with exact precision, but it is time-consuming. Generally, if an item cost is < $0.10 per serving, there is a cost-/time-beneficial way to add costs for these small ingredients to a recipe. Chapter 10 discusses further how to account for herb, spice, and seasoning cost when determining the cost of a recipe or cost per portion to serve a guest.

 ## The Difference between the EP and AS Portion

As mentioned in the previous chapter, the term edible portion means the total yield of a recipe, or a fully cooked item. For example, a rib roast is the total amount of edible product available to serve the guest.

EP EXAMPLE

The recipe yields a pan of lasagna.

The pan of lasagna is the EP.

or

A fully cooked rib roast weighs 10 pounds.

The 10 pounds is the EP.

Food is as served to the guest in a specific-size portion. Most recipes yield more than one portion. The entire edible portion is not served to the guest. A portion or percent of the recipe is AS to the guest.

AS EXAMPLE

The pan of lasagna is cut into 24 portions.

The lasagna is AS in a portion that is $\frac{1}{24}$ of the entire EP.

or

The fully cooked rib roast is carved into 6-ounce portions.

The rib roast is AS in 6-ounce portions carved from the EP of 10 pounds.

The exception would be to AP portion-controlled items. Portion-controlled items are the EP and AS portion.

 ## The Difference between the EP and AS Cost

There can be a cost variation between the EP cost and the AS cost. Anytime the entire EP cannot be evenly divided into an AS portion, the cost per portion increases. This happens most often with meats that are roasted.

EDIBLE PORTION (EP) AND AS SERVED (AS) COST VARIATION EXAMPLE

The EP of a rib roast is 10 pounds.

The AS portion size is 6 ounces.

The EP in ounces is as follows:

10 (pounds) × 16 (ounces per pound) = 160 EP ounces

The number of AS portions is as follows:

160 (EP ounces) ÷ 6 (AS portion in ounces) = 26.67 portions

The total AS portions is 26.

The .67 of a portion cannot be served.

The .67 of a portion is EP that is too small to be AS to a guest. The cost of this EP is absorbed by the cost of the 26 portions served.

AS SERVED COST PER PORTION EXAMPLE

The EP cost for the 10-pound roast is $35.00.

The AS number of portions is 26.

The cost per AS portion is as follows:

$35.00 (cost for roast) ÷ 26 (AS portions) = $1.346 rounded to $1.35 cost per AS portion

The cost per AS portion is $1.35.

The variance between the EP and the AS portion is a factor that you should understand and consider when purchasing, determining the portion cost, and when pricing a menu.

Conclusion

The different food product groups and their corresponding AP and EP yields need to be understood and considered each time a food item is purchased. Each choice made has an impact on EP and/or AS quantity and cost. The food product choices made directly impact profitability, the culinary staff, and the customers.

Foodservice-Specific Mathematics: Part II REVIEW PROBLEMS

1. *Food product groups.* List the specific food groups that have a yield variance between their AP state and their EP state.

2. What factors or conditions create a yield variance between AP weight and EP weight? Give specific examples.

3. What factors or conditions create a yield variance between EP weight and AS weight? Give an example.

4. Which food product groups have a 100% yield?

5. Which food product groups have a yield percent greater than (>) 100%?

6. What does the term *fabrication* mean?

7. What is the difference between a portion-controlled meat and a non-portion-controlled meat product in terms of:

   a. AP weight vs. EP weight

   b. AP price vs. EP price

   c. EP weight vs. AS weight

   d. EP price vs. AS price

Yield Test Review Problem

AP rib primal

AP weight 35 pounds

AP price per pound $2.09

a. What is the total AP cost for the rib primal?

After Fabrication	(×)	Market Value	(=)	Total Value
20-pound oven-ready rib roast		$3.99 per pound		
4 pounds stew beef		$1.99 per pound		
5 pounds short ribs		$1.59 per pound		
3 pounds beef bones		$0.55 per pound		
3 pounds beef fat		$0.07 per pound		

b. Fill in the total market value per item column

c. What is the total market value for the entire rib primal? (total of rib roast and by-products)

d. What is the yield percent for the rib roast from the rib primal?

e. What is the total yield for all of the by-products?

f. What is the cost of the oven-ready rib roast fabricated from the rib primal? (Remember to subtract the market value of the by-products.)

g. What is the market value of a 20-pound oven-ready rib roast?

h. Which product should be purchased, the rib primal or the oven-ready roast? Why?

CHAPTER 10

Foodservice-Specific Terminology *and* Mathematics

Part III
Recipe and Portion Costing

> *"A survey of 300 restaurant chefs around the country reveals that looks, cost, and customer expectations are what matters whey they determine portion size."*
>
> —MARILYNN MARCHIONE, WRITER, *ASSOCIATED PRESS*

As discussed in Chapter 9, the edible portion (EP) of any food item is the actual product that is available to serve a guest. The as served (AS) portion is the exact amount of a food that is actually served to the guest on the plate. The cost of the EP is determined by the as purchased (AP) cost of the item and its yield percent. The AS portion cost is determined by the EP cost and the weight or volume of the AS portion size. This information is vital in order to determine the cost of preparing a recipe and the cost of serving a portion of food to a guest.

LEARNING OBJECTIVES

1. To review the relationship between AP cost and EP cost
2. To understand and use the approximate or average yield percent for food items
3. To understand the nine-step process used to cost a recipe
4. To understand the process used to determine the cost of an AS portion
5. To understand the impact of portion size on an AS cost

A Review of the Relationship between AP and EP

Food items are AP in a specific unit of measure and cost per unit of measure. As the food items are prepared for service, their AP unit of measure becomes an EP unit of measure. The EP unit of measure generally has a different cost per unit than the AP unit cost.

This difference between the AP and EP unit cost is the result of the yield percent.

YIELD PERCENT FORMULAS

To determine product yield:

$$\text{Yield percent} = \frac{\text{EP weight (or volume)}}{\text{AP weight (or volume)}}$$

To determine the correct amount of product to order:

$$\text{AP quantity} = \frac{\text{EP weight (or volume)}}{\text{Yield percent}}$$

To determine the actual cost of the food served to the guest:

$$\text{EP or AS price} = \frac{\text{AP price per unit}}{\text{Yield percent}}$$

Approximate or Average Yield Percent

Chapters 8 and 9 discussed the meaning and impact of a food item's/food group's yield percent. The yield percent has a direct impact on the food item's/food group's EP weight/volume and on the food item's/food group's EP and AS cost per portion. Because of the importance of this information, and the fact that a food item's/food group's yield percents can be fairly consistent, **approximate** or **average yield percent** for different food items/food groups have been developed.

Appendix III is a list of commonly used food items and their approximate or average yield percent. In Appendix III, for example, a large onion has a 91% yield. This information is valuable because it saves a great deal of time when you are determining AP weight/volume of products, measuring ingredients for a recipe, or developing the total cost of a recipe.

These measurements are approximate and may be very different than what you encounter in your kitchen. They are valuable to use as a learning tool to practice the mathematics for determining purchasing quantity and EP cost, but they may not apply to your professional kitchen.

QUICK TIP: A yield test can be performed on any food product in your kitchen. The item is measured (weighed/volume) in its AP state, and again it its EP state. EP/AP = yield percent. This is the only way to ensure the yield percent is indeed correct for your kitchen.

Recipe Costing Examples Using Approximate or Average Yield Percents

Following is an example using the onions mentioned in the previous section and the approximate or average yield percent information to assist with finding the cost of onion in a recipe. The form used is a standardized recipe cost form, which is located in Appendix IV. This form is set up so the information from a standardized recipe form can be transferred to this standardized cost form. The column headings explain the steps to take to arrive at the ingredient's costs. The approximate or average yield percent information is available in Appendix III. This form provides an easy-to-follow format to determine the cost to prepare a particular recipe.

The accuracy of the recipe's cost will depend on the accuracy of the yield percents used and the number of decimal places used in your calculations. Four decimal places, to the ten-thousandth place, should be sufficient to produce a fairly accurate cost per recipe ingredient. Rounding to two decimal places, to the hundredth place, can be done *after* all of the calculations are completed and the recipe is totaled. The total recipe cost is then divided by the number of portions the recipe serves to determine a cost per portion.

EXAMPLE USING LARGE ONIONS

AP cost per pound = $.69

Average yield percent = 91%, or .91

This recipe example uses 12 ounces of large onion. The AP cost per pound is $.69, and the average yield percent is 91%. The EP price per pound is $.76. This recipe only uses 12 ounces, not 16 ounces, so the cost for the 12 ounces is $.57.

STANDARDIZED RECIPE COST FORM

Item Name

Recipe Yield: **Total Cost:**
Portion Size: **Cost per Portion:**
Number of Portions: **Date:**

Item	Item Quantity	AP Unit of Measure	AP Cost per Unit	÷	Average Yield Percent (or Other Unit of Measure Info)	=	EP Cost per Unit	×	Item Quantity	=	Recipe Item Cost
Onions, Large	12 ounces EP	Pounds	$.69	÷	91%, or .91	=	.7582, or .76	×	12 ounces, or .75 pound	=	.5687, or .57

The Nine Steps to Calculate a Recipe's Cost

The preceding onion example is a simplified version of the process used to cost an entire recipe. The following is a list of the nine steps necessary to accurately determine the cost of a recipe. From this information, the portion cost of a menu item can also be determined.

The steps to calculating a recipe cost are as follows:

STEP 1: Refer to a blank standardized recipe cost form (Appendix IV).

STEP 2: Transfer the ingredients, quantities, and recipe yield from a standardized recipe form, and place the date on the cost form.

STEP 3: Transfer the AP unit of measure and AP price per unit from the purveyor's invoice(s).

STEP 4: Look up each ingredient's

1. Approximate or average yield percent (or perform a yield test)

2. Unit of measure conversion if the AP unit is different than the recipe unit of measure

3. Unit of measure conversion for item AP by count, bunch, and so on

> STEP 5: Perform the calculations to four decimal places to first determine the EP cost per unit.
>
> STEP 6: Then determine the EP cost for the total number of units in the recipe.
>
> STEP 7: Add each ingredient cost to arrive at a recipe cost.
>
> STEP 8: Multiply the recipe cost by 102%, or 1.02, to add in the cost of miscellaneous ingredients.*
>
> STEP 9: Divide the total recipe cost by the number of portions it yields to determine the actual cost per portion.*
>
> *The total cost can be rounded here or after the per portion cost.

CALCULATING A RECIPE'S COST: SIMPLE EXAMPLE

This recipe is for cream of broccoli soup. The ingredients have been transferred to the standardized recipe cost form from a standardized recipe form (not shown). The only ingredient that has a yield variance is the onion. We will use the onion from the prior example.

This recipe for cream of broccoli soup is easy to cost because all of ingredients, except the onion, have a 100% yield. This means the AP cost per unit is equal to the EP cost per unit. Therefore, the amount of the item used in the recipe is multiplied by the AP cost, and the item's total recipe cost is the product. After all of the individual items' costs are determined, they are added together to find the recipe's total cost. The cost per portion is determined by dividing the total recipe cost by the number of portions it serves.

In this example, the total cost to make 6 quarts of cream of broccoli soup is $11.3388, rounded to $11.34. Soup can be served by the cup or the bowl. The cup holds 4 ounces, and the bowl holds 8 ounces. The total portions that can be served from this recipe are as follows:

> Total edible product ÷ Portion size = Number of portions
>
> 6 quarts = 6 (quarts) × 32 (ounces per quart) = 192 ounces
>
> 192 ounces ÷ 4 ounces (per cup) = 48 cups
>
> or
>
> 192 ounces ÷ 8 ounces (per bowl) = 24 bowls

The cost for an AS portion from this recipe is as follows:

> Total recipe cost ÷ Number of AS portions = Cost per AS portion
>
> The cost for a cup of soup is as follows:
>
> $11.34 (total recipe cost) ÷ 48 (cups) = .2362 rounded to $0.24.
>
> The cost for a bowl of soup is as follows:
>
> $11.34 (total recipe cost) ÷ 24 = .4725 rounded to $0.47.

STANDARDIZED RECIPE COST FORM

Cream of Broccoli Soup

Recipe Yield: 6 quarts (192 ounces)   **Total Cost:** $11.34/ **Cost per Quart:** $1.89

Portion Size: Cup: 4 ounces/Bowl: 8 ounces   **Cost Per Portion:** Cup: .24 Bowl: .47

Number of Portions: Cups: 48 Bowls: 24   **Date:** June 20XX

Item	Item Quantity	AP Unit of Measure	AP Cost per Unit	÷	Average Yield Percent (or Other Unit of Measure Info)	=	EP Cost per Unit	×	Item Quantity	=	Recipe Item Cost
Chicken Stock	4.5 qts.	Quart	$.70	÷	100%	=	.70	×	4.5	=	$3.15
Broccoli	3 pounds	Pound	$1.09	÷	100%	=	1.09	×	3	=	$3.27
Onion, Large	12 ounces	Pound	$.69	÷	91%	=	.7582	×	.75 pound*	=	$.5687
Butter	9 ounces	Pound	$2.50	÷	100%	=	2.50	×	.56 pound*	=	$1.4063
Flour	9 ounces	Pound	$.50	÷	100%	=	.50	×	.56 pound*	=	$.2813
Milk	1.5 qts.	Quart	$.65	÷	100%	=	.65	×	1.5	=	$.9750
Cream	3 cups	Quart	$2.25	÷	100%	=	2.25	×	.75*	=	$1.6875

Total recipe cost = $11.3388, rounded to $11.34

*Item quantities are converted to decimal numbers. It is easier to multiply a decimal.

Onion: 12 ounces/16 ounces (pound) = .75 pound; butter: 9 ounces/16 ounces (pound) = .56 pound;

Flour: 9 ounces/16 ounces (pound) = .56 pound; cream: 3 cups/4 cups (quart) = .75 quart.

The AS cost for a cup of soup is $0.24, and the AS cost for a bowl of soup is $0.47.

CALCULATING A RECIPE'S COST: COMMON EXAMPLE— YIELD PERCENT AND SEASONINGS

This recipe is for beef stew. The recipe uses beef chuck, cubed, a variety of vegetables, seasonings, and beef stock. The quantities and ingredients are transferred from a standardized recipe form. The AP cost per unit is found on the food purveyor's invoice. The yield percents are from the approximate or average yield percent list in Appendix III. The cost for seasonings is a miscellaneous cost. This miscellaneous cost is considered to be an additional 2% of the recipe cost. Once totaled, the recipe cost is multiplied by 1.02% or 1.02 (the decimal equivalent). The product is the total recipe cost.

> Recipe cost × 1.02% or 1.02 = Total recipe cost

Once the total recipe cost is calculated, the cost per portion is calculated. The cost per portion is calculated by dividing the recipe cost by the number of portions the recipe yields.

> Total recipe cost ÷ Number of portions = Cost per portion

The ingredients for the beef stew recipe total $19.29. The total recipe cost, with the 2% for miscellaneous ingredients, is as follows:

> $19.29 × 1.02 = $19.6758, rounded to $19.68

The beef stew recipe yields (serves) 20 portions. The actual cost per portion is as follows:

> $19.68 (total recipe cost) ÷ 20 (number of portions) = $0.9840, rounded to $0.99 (or $1.00 per portion)

Miscellaneous Ingredient Cost Explained

The 2 percent miscellaneous ingredient cost added to the recipe cost is a cost-/time-beneficial way to add the cost of ordinary seasonings, small amounts of oil, and so on used in a recipe. As mentioned in Chapter 9, the cost of miscellaneous ingredients can be precisely determined, but it is time-consuming.

If the beef stew recipe uses 2 T of salt and 2 T of black pepper, what is the actual additional cost for these items? Both of these seasonings are purchased by the ounce but measured by the tablespoon, so the AP units of measure need to be converted into EP units of measure.

> Salt is AP by the pound.
>
> AP price per pound = $0.20
>
> AP price per pound is $.20 ÷ 16 (ounces per pound) = $.0125 per ounce
>
> 2 T of salt = Approximately 1 ounce
>
> The cost for the salt is < 2 pennies.
>
> Black pepper is AP by the pound.
>
> AP price per pound = $12.00
>
> AP price per pound = $12.00 ÷ 16 (ounces per pound) = $.75 per ounce
>
> 2 T of black pepper = $\frac{1}{2}$, .50, or 50% of an ounce
>
> The cost for the black pepper is $.375, or 38 cents.

Beef Stew

Recipe Yield: 1.25 gallons (160 fl. oz.)   **Total Cost: $19.68**

Portion Size: 8 fl. oz.   **Cost per Portion: $.99 ($19.68/20 = .9840)**

Number of Portions: 20 (160/8 = 20)   **Date: June 20XX**

Item	Item Quantity	AP Unit of Measure	AP Cost per Unit	÷	Average Yield Percent (or Other Unit of Measure Info)	=	EP Cost per Unit	×	Item Quantity	=	Recipe Item Cost
Beef, chuck, cubed	AP 8.5 pounds	Pounds	$1.25	÷	100% or 1.00	=	1.25 per pound	×	8.5 pounds	=	$10.6250
Onion, diced	EP 2 pounds	Pounds	$.39	÷	91% or .91	=	.4286 per pound	×	2 pounds	=	$.8571
Carrots, baby	EP 4 pounds	Pounds	$.79	÷	99% or .99	=	.7980 per pound	×	4 pounds	=	$3.1919
Celery	EP 2 pounds	Bunch (32 AP ounces per bunch)	$1.25	÷	68.8% or .688	=	1.8169 per 32 EP ounces	×	1 bunch (32 EP ounces)	=	$1.8169
Beef stock	4 quarts	Quart	$.70	÷	100% or 1.00	=	.70	×	4 qts.	=	$2.80

Recipe cost = $19.2909

Recipe cost plus 2% for misc. items = $ 19.29
× 1.02

$19.6758 rounded to $19.68

The total cost for the salt and black pepper is rounded to $0.40. The total for the 2% miscellaneous ingredient cost is $0.39. The difference is $0.01.

The cost of labor involved in costing out the salt and pepper is far greater than the $.01 difference. Therefore, the 2% for miscellaneous ingredients cost is a cost-/labor-effective way to add those costs to recipes.

 QUICK TIP: There are some seasonings and spices, such as vanilla beans, pure vanilla, and saffron, to name a few, that are very expensive. If the cost of the seasoning is high, then it must be calculated and added to the recipe cost as an item. If it is a low-cost spice or seasoning, the 2% rule works well.

❀ Additional Cost to Serve a Guest a Meal

Based on our beef stew example, the actual cost for an 8-fl. oz. portion of beef stew is $0.99 (or $1.00). There may also be other items served to the guest in addition to the beef stew. Many restaurants offer a choice of soup or salad with an entrée, and rolls and butter are typically served. These additional items also need to have a cost per portion, so the actual total cost to serve a guest a meal can be identified.

If the average cost to serve soup or salad to a guest is $0.80, and the average cost for rolls and butter is $0.20, then the total cost to serve a guest a beef stew entrée is as follows:

> $1.00 (beef stew) + $0.80 (soup/salad) + $0.20 (rolls and butter) = $2.00
> Total cost to serve the guest the beef stew entrée.

The total cost to serve a meal to the guest must be considered when determining the menu prices. This topic is covered in Chapter 11.

❀ Conclusion

Accurate recipe and portion costing are critical to the success and profitability of a restaurant. The mathematics include basic addition, multiplication, and division. The information needed to calculate the cost of a recipe and an AS portion cost is listed on the standardized recipe form, the invoices from the restaurant's food purveyors, and the approximate or average yield percent list (see Appendix III), or yield percents developed in your professional kitchen. This information is then transferred to the standardized recipe cost form. The calculations are completed and the ingredient costs are totaled. Recipe costs and AS portion cost are two pieces of the profit puzzle for the foodservice industry.

Foodservice-Specific Mathematics: Part III REVIEW PROBLEMS

1. List the information contained in a standardized recipe.

2. What information from a standardized recipe is used to calculate a recipe's cost?

3. What additional information is required to calculate a recipe's cost?

4. What information is required to calculate a portion cost?

Complete the following standardized recipe cost forms to determine the total recipe cost and the cost per portion.

STANDARDIZED RECIPE COST FORM

8-ounces Rib Eye with Sautéed Mushrooms

Recipe Yield: 1 portion
Portion Size: 8-ounce rib eye; .25 pound mushrooms
Number of Portions: 1

Total Cost:
Cost per Portion:
Date:

Item	Item Quantity	AP Unit of Measure	AP Cost per Unit	÷	Average Yield Percent (or Other Unit of Measure Info)	=	EP Cost per Unit	×	Item Quantity	=	Recipe Item Cost
8-ounce rib eye	1 each	Pound (16 ounces)	$6.99 (per pound)		AP = 2 per pound	=		×		=	
Mush	.25 pound	Pound	2.50 (per pound)	÷	93.8%, or .938	=		×		=	
Wine	1 ounce	Milliliter	5.00 Per 750 mL		750mL = 25.4 fl. oz.	=		×		=	
									Recipe cost	=	

Recipe Cost Plus 2% for Misc. Items   **Total recipe cost =**

STANDARDIZED RECIPE COST FORM

Baked Crusted Tuna

Recipe Yield: 26 pounds
Portion Size: 8 ounces
Number of Portions: 52

Total Cost:
Cost per Portion:
Date:

Item	Item Quantity	AP Unit of Measure	AP Cost per Unit	÷	Average Yield Percent (or Other Unit of Measure Info)	=	EP Cost per Unit	×	Item Quantity	=	Recipe Item Cost
Tuna, dressed	26 EP pounds	Pound	5.99	÷	65%, or .65	=		×		=	
Olive oil	1 C	L	2.39		1 C = 237 mL	=		×		=	
Fresh lemon juice	1 qt.	Pound	.79		(2 C = 1 pound)	=		×		=	
Bread crumbs	1 gallon	Pound	.59		(2 qts. = 1 pound)	=		×		=	
Fish stock	.5 gallon	Qt.	1.29			=		×		=	
Parsley	5 ounces	Pound	12.50			=		×		=	
									Recipe cost	=	

Recipe Cost Plus 2% for Misc. Items   Total recipe cost =

Running Case Study

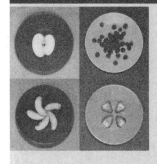

Step IV

Thomas has been learning about the difference between as purchased, edible portion, and as served. He realizes that he needs to cost the recipes he is going to use in his restaurant. He also realizes that he needs to determine a cost per portion for each of his menu items.

Standardized Recipe #1

The Best Meatballs Ever

Preparation and Cooking Time: 1.5 hours **Recipe Yield: 60 Each**
Portion Size: 2 each **Number of Portions: 30**

Quantity	Ingredients	Preparation Method
5 pounds	Ground beef	
5 pounds	Ground pork	
10 cups	Italian bread crumbs	
10 each	Eggs	
	Recipe served 30 portions.	
	To serve 50 portions:	
	New/Old = Multiplier	
	50/30 = 1.67	
5 pounds × 1.67 = 8.3 pounds	Ground beef	
5 pounds × 1.67 = 8.3 pounds	Ground pork	
10 cups × 1.67 = 16.7 cups	Italian bread crumbs	
10 eggs × 1.67 = 16.7	Eggs	
	Correct Units of Measure	
8.3 pounds (weight)	Ground beef	
8.3 pounds (weight)	Ground pork	
3.13 pounds (weight, not volume)	Italian bread crumbs	
17 each (count, rounded from 16.7 to 17)	Eggs	

Standardized Recipe Cost Form

The Best Meatballs Ever

Recipe Yield: 60 each **Total Cost:** $35.11
Portion Size: 2 each **Cost per Portion:** $1.1703, rounded to $1.17
Number of Portions: 30 **Date:** June 20XX

Item	Item Quantity	AP Unit of Measure	AP Cost per Unit	÷	Average Yield Percent (or Other Unit of Measure Info)	=	EP Cost per Unit	×	Item Quantity	=	Recipe Item Cost
Beef, ground	8.3 pounds	Pounds	$1.79	÷	100%	=	$1.79	×	8.3 pounds	=	$14.857
Pork, ground	8.3 pounds	Pounds	$1.99	÷	100%	=	$1.99	×	8.3 pounds	=	$16.517
Bread crumbs	3.13 pounds	Pounds	.65	÷	100%	=	.65	×	3.13	=	$2.0345
Eggs	17 each	Dozen	1.20	÷	12 (per dozen)	=	.10	×	17	=	$1.70
								Total Recipe Cost		=	$35.1085, rounded to $35.11

Thomas has determined the total cost to prepare 60 meatballs is $35.11. The cost per portion is $1.17.

Standardized Recipe #2

Beef Braised in Red Wine Sauce

Preparation and Cooking Time: 3.5 hours　　**Recipe Yield:**
Portion Size:　　**Number of Portions: 6**

Quantity	Ingredients	Preparation Method
2 T	Vegetable oil	
4 pound	Beef roast	
1 T	Butter	
3 T	Yellow onion, chopped	
2 T	Carrot, chopped	
2 T	Celery, chopped	
1.5 cups	Dry red wine	
1 cup	Beef stock	
1.5 T	Italian tomatoes	
Pinch	Thyme	
1/8 tsp.	Marjoram	
	Recipe served 6 portions.	
	To serve 50 portions:	
	New/Old = Multiplier	
	50/6 = 8.3	
2 T × 8.3 = 16.67 T	Vegetable oil	
4 pounds × 8.3 = 33.2 pounds	Beef roast	
1 T × 8.3 = 8.3 T	Butter	
3 T × 8.3 = 24.9 T	Yellow onion, chopped	
2 T × 8.3 = 16.6 T	Carrot, chopped	
2 T × 8.3 = 16.6 T	Celery, chopped	
1.5 cups × 8.3 = 12.45 cups	Dry red wine	
1 cup × 8.3 = 8.3 cups	Beef stock	
1.5 T × 8.3 = 12.45 T	Italian tomatoes	
Pinch × 8.3 = ?	Thyme	
1/8 tsp. × 8.3 = 1 tsp.	Marjoram	
	Correct Units of Measure	
1 cup, 2 tsp. (volume)	Vegetable oil	
33.2 pounds (weight)	Beef roast	
4 ounces (weight)	Butter	
12 ounces (weight)	Yellow onion, chopped	
4 ounces (weight)	Carrot, chopped	
4 ounces (weight)	Celery, chopped	
3 quarts, 1/2 cup (volume)	Dry red wine	
2 quarts, 3 fl. oz. (volume)	Beef stock	
6 ounces (weight)	Italian tomatoes	
1 tsp. (volume)	Thyme	
1 tsp. (volume)	Marjoram	

Standardized Recipe Cost Form

Beef Braised in Red Wine Sauce

Recipe Yield: 25 pounds
Portion Size: 8 ounces
Number of Portions: 50

Total Cost: $91.24
Cost per Portion: $1.8248/$1.83
Date: June 20XX

Item	Item Quantity	AP Unit of Measure	AP Cost per Unit	÷	Average Yield Percent (or Other Unit of Measure Info)	=	EP Cost per Unit	×	Item Quantity	=	Recipe Item Cost
Vegetable oil	1 cup + 2 tsp. (.33 fl. oz.)	Quart	4.00		1 C = .25 qt. + .33 fl. oz.	=	1.00	×	1 cup 2 tsp.	=	$1.0413
Beef, roast	33.2 pounds	Pound	2.29		Entire roast is used.	=	2.29	×	33.2 pounds	=	$76.0280
Butter	4 ounces	Pound	2.50		4 ounces = .25 pound	=	.1563 per ounce	×	4 ounces	=	$.6250
Onion	12 ounces	Pound	.69	÷	91%, or .91	=	.7582 pound	×	.75 pound	=	$.5687
Carrot	4 ounces	Pound	.59	÷	82%, or .82	=	.7195 pound	×	.25 pound	=	$.1799
Celery	4 ounces	Bunch (2 pounds)	.99	÷	69%, or .69	=	1.4348 pounds	×	.125 b	=	$.1793
Red wine	3.125 quarts	Liter	3.00		Quarts to liters 3.125 × .946 = 2.96 L	=	3.00	×	2.96	=	$8.88
Beef stock	2.09 quarts	Quart	.70		100%	=	.70	×	2.09	=	$1.4630
Italian tomatoes	6 ounces (can)	Pound	1.29		100%	=	1.29	×	.375 pounds	=	$.4838
Thyme	.5 tsp.	Ounce	2.00		Misc.		Cost			=	2%
Marjoram	1 tsp.	Ounce	2.00		Misc.		Cost			=	2%

Total Recipe Cost = $89.449

Misc. Cost   × 1.02

Total Recipe Cost = $91.238
$91.24

Standardized Recipe #3

Veal Scaloppine with Lemon Saunce

Preparation and Cooking Time: 5 min.
Portion Size: .25 pound

Recipe Yield:
Number of Portions: 4

Quantity	Ingredients	Preparation Method
2 T	Vegetable oil	
1/4 cup	Butter	
1 pound	Veal, pounded flat	
3/4 cup	Flour	
2 T	Lemon juice	
2 T	Parsley, chopped	
1/2	Lemon, sliced	
	Recipe served 4 portions.	
	To serve 50 portions:	
	New/Old = Multiplier	
	50/4 = 12.5	
2 T × 12.5 = 25 T	Vegetable oil	
1/4 cup × 12.5 = 3.125 cups	Butter	
1 pound × 12.5 = 12.5 pounds	Veal, pounded flat	
3/4 cup × 12.5 = 9.375 cup	Flour	
2 T × 12.5 = 25 T	Lemon juice	
2 T × 12.5 = 25 T	Parsley, chopped	
1/2 × 12.5 = 6.25	Lemon, sliced	
	Correct Units of Measure	
1½ cups plus 1 T (volume)	Vegetable oil	
1½ pounds (weight)	Butter	
12.5 pounds (weight)	Veal, pounded flat	
2.34 pounds (weight)	Flour	
1½ cups plus 1 T (volume)	Lemon juice	
1½ cups plus 1 T (volume)	Parsley, chopped	
6¼ each (count)	Lemon, sliced	

Standardized Recipe Cost Form

Veal Scaloppine with Lemon Sauce

Recipe Yield: 10 pounds   Total Cost: $84.48

Portion Size: 3.2 ounces   Cost per Portion: $1.6896/$1.69

Number of Portions: 50   Date: June 20XX

Item	Item Quantity	AP Unit of Measure	AP Cost per Unit ÷	Average Yield Percent (or Other Unit of Measure Info) =	EP Cost per Unit ×	Item Quantity =	Recipe Item Cost
Vegetable oil	1.5 C + 1 T	Quart	4.00	1.5 C + 1 T = .39 qt.	4.00	× .39 qt	= $1.56
Butter	1.5 pounds	Pound	2.50	100%	2.50	× 1.5 pounds	= $3.75
Veal	12.5 pounds	Pound	5.99	Portion-control item	5.99	× 12.5 pounds	= $74.875
Flour	2.34 pounds	Pound	.50	100%	.50	× 2.34 pounds	= $1.170
Lemon juice	1.5 C + 1 T	Quart	1.75	.39 qt.	1.75	× .39	= $.6825
Parsley	1.5 C + 1 T	Bunch* *(6-ounce wt.)	1.25	1.8 ounces = 1 C: Total need 2.7 ounces	1 ounce, = .21	× 2.7 ounces	= $.5670
Lemon sliced	6.25 each	Each	.30		.30	× 6.25	= $1.875
					Total Recipe Cost =		$84.4795 $84.48

Thomas has determined the cost for the three main entrée items he would like to serve at *Tomas*, his restaurant. The cost per portion is not the entire AS cost because additional items are served with a meal. Thomas will add those additional items to his recipe portion costs in the next section of the text.

The cost for the three recipes you have written needs to be calculated. Current prices can be obtained on a visit to a local grocery store, or you can call a local food purveyor. Remember, the approximate or average yield percent list is in Appendix III and the standardized recipe cost form is in Appendix IV.

MATHEMATICS *for the* BUSINESS SIDE *of the* FOODSERVICE INDUSTRY

CHAPTER 11

Menu Pricing

"The toughest decision made in a foodservice operation is how much to charge for the product and service. The price must offer value to the guest, and profit to the business."

—TERRI JONES

Menu pricing is a complicated business decision. The actual food cost of an item is one of many factors to consider in assigning a menu price. One method often used to price a menu is called **food cost percent pricing**. This particular method analyzes the cost of the food and a predetermined food cost percent to develop the menu price. This method is where we begin our discussion on menu pricing.

LEARNING OBJECTIVES

1. To develop an understanding of the different strategies used in menu pricing: à la carte, table d'hôte, and prix fixe
2. To define the terms **food cost** and **food cost percent**
3. To understand the relationship between food cost, food cost percent, and a menu price
4. To understand the limitations of food cost percent pricing
5. To explore other menu pricing techniques
6. To develop an understanding of beverage cost and beverage cost percent
7. To understand the pricing techniques used in the sale of alcoholic beverages
8. To develop an understanding of the pricing techniques used in the baking and pastry industry

À la Carte, Table d' Hôte, and Prix Fixe

The U.S. foodservice industry uses two different menu pricing strategies. The first pricing strategy is called **à la carte**. À la carte pricing assigns an individual price to every item on the menu. When a guest orders from an à la carte menu, there is a separate charge for every item ordered. À la carte pricing is often found in upscale casual and fine-dining restaurants. This pricing strategy tends to increase the average guest check. The menu that follows is an example of an à la carte menu.

À LA CARTE MENU EXAMPLE

Steak	$21.95
Chicken	$16.95
Fish	$27.95

VEGETABLES

Broccoli	$7.95
Asparagus	$8.95
Baked potato	$6.95

SALADS

Dinner salad	$3.95
Spinach salad	$6.95
House special salad	$8.95

When a guest orders an entrée from an à la carte menu, the plate only has the steak, chicken, or fish on it. If you would like a salad before the entrée, there is an additional charge. It is not included in the price of the entrée. The same is true for a vegetable. If you would like a vegetable served with your entrée, there is an additional charge. It is not included in the price of the entrée.

The second pricing strategy used in the United States is called **table d'hôte** or **prix fixe**. A **table d'hôte** or **prix fixe** menu prices an entire meal at one price. A table d'hôte meal generally includes a choice of soup or salad and an entrée with a vegetable and a starch for one price. This menu pricing strategy is found in mid-scale and casual restaurants. It can also be found in the quick-serve (fast-food) industry and often includes a drink.

A prix fixe menu is similar to a table d'hôte menu. A prix fixe menu generally includes the entire meal, including a dessert course, for one price. Tasting menus in fine-dining restaurants are often prix fixe. Following is an example of a table d'hôte menu.

TABLE D'HÔTE MENU EXAMPLE

Entrées

All entrées are served with choice of soup or salad, rolls and butter, and two of the following:

French fries, baked potato, rice, vegetable of the day, fresh fruit, or sliced tomatoes.

Steak	$12.95
Chicken	$9.95
Fish	$15.95

When a guest orders an entrée from a table d'hôte menu, the soup or salad, and two side dishes are included in the entrée price.

 **Food Cost**

The term **food cost** refers to the actual cost of the food that is served to the guest. In a restaurant that uses the table d'hôte or prix fixe pricing strategy, the total cost of the entire meal is considered to be the food cost.

FOOD COST PERCENT

The term "**food cost percent**" refers to the percent of the menu price that the cost of the food represents. If the cost of the food is $2.50 and the menu price is $10.00, the food cost percent is 25% because $2.50 is 25% of $10.00. The 25% food cost percent means that every time the $10.00 menu item is sold, $2.50 of the $10.00 pays for the cost of the food and $7.50 is available to pay for the other costs of doing business and the profit.

FOOD COST, FOOD COST PERCENT, AND MENU PRICING

One common method for pricing a menu involves using the cost of the food and a predetermined food cost percent. The following three formulas are used for this method of pricing a menu.

FOOD COST/ MENU PRICING FORMULAS

Formula I

The cost of the food and the food cost percent are known:

Food cost ÷ Food cost percent = Menu price

Formula II

The menu price and the food cost percent are known:

Menu price × Food cost percent = Food cost

Formula III

The cost of the food and the menu price are known:

Food cost ÷ Menu price × 100* = Food cost percent

*Multiplying the quotient by 100 changes the decimal to a percent.

FOOD COST/MENU PRICING EXAMPLE

Formula I

The cost of the food and the food cost percent are known.

The cost to serve a hamburger on a bun with lettuce and tomato is $0.60.

The predetermined food cost percent is 25%.

The formula is

Food cost ÷ Food cost percent = Menu price

$0.60 ÷ 25% (or .25 as a decimal) = $2.40

The menu price is $2.40.

Formula II

The menu price and the food cost percent are known.

The menu price is $2.40.

The food cost percent is 25%.

The formula is

Menu price × Food cost percent = Food cost

$2.40 × 25% (or .25 as a decimal) = $0.60

The cost of the food is $0.60.

Formula III

The cost of the food and the menu price are known.

The food costs $0.60.

The menu price is $2.40.

The formula is

Food cost ÷ Menu price × 100 = Food cost percent

$0.60 ÷ $2.40 = .25 × 100 = 25%

The food cost percent is 25%.

Formula I: Food Cost ÷ Food Cost Percent = Menu Price

Formula I is used when the food cost and the food cost percent are known. A foodservice operator should know exactly what his food costs are. Then he can decide on a predetermined food cost percent that he uses to price his menu. If the cost of the food is $3.65 and he wants to run a 30% food cost, what will the menu price be?

$3.65 ÷ 30% (or .30 as a decimal) = $12.1667 rounded to $12.17

In this example, the menu price is $12.17 based on a $3.65 food cost and a 30% food cost percent.

Formula II: Menu Price × Food Cost Percent = Food Cost

Formula II is used when the menu price and the food cost percent are known. A foodservice operator decides that entrées priced between $10.00 and $20.00 provide value to his customers. This is the menu price range. He also decides his food cost percent should be 30%. How much should his food cost?

For a $10.00 menu item: $10.00 × 30% (or .30 as a decimal) = $3.00
The food cost should be $3.00.

For a $20.00 menu item: $20.00 × 30% (or .30 as a decimal) = $6.00
The food cost should be $6.00.

This foodservice operator should have menu items with a food cost of $3.00 to $6.00.

This way, he can offer value to his customers and maintain a food cost percent of 30%.

Formula III: Food Cost ÷ Menu Price × 100 = Food Cost Percent

Formula III is used when the cost of the food and the menu price are known. The foodservice operator knows that his food cost is $3.65 and his menu price is $12.17. He wants to know what his food cost percent is.

$3.65 ÷ $12.17 = .2999 rounded to .30 × 100 = 30%

His food cost percent is 30%.

These three formulas are the basis for food cost percentage menu pricing. This method of pricing is common, with some adjustments. In the example above, the menu price is $12.17. This is not the typical price you commonly see on a menu. The price is generally adjusted to a more consumer-accepted number, such as $12.95. Adjusting the menu price does change the actual food cost percent.

$$\$3.65 \div \$12.95 = .2819 \text{ rounded to } 28\%$$

The adjusted food cost percent is 28%.

Limitations of Food Cost Percentage Pricing

Food cost percentage pricing does have limitations. It is based on the premise that the cost of the food is a certain percentage of the menu price and the remaining money collected from the sale of the food will pay for the other costs of doing business and the profit. In the preceding example, the menu price is $12.95 and the cost of the food is $3.65. The money left from the sale of this item is as follows:

$$\$12.95 - \$3.65 = \$9.30$$

Every time this item is sold, the restaurant has $9.30 to cover the other costs of doing business and the profit. This method of pricing will not produce a profit for every operation.

The cost of doing business and the profit motive for a fine-dining or upscale casual restaurant in a high-rent district, with a chef and a highly skilled culinary team and with high labor costs, cannot rely on food cost percent pricing to cover these costs. It relies on different pricing methods.

Additional Menu Pricing Techniques

One of the best menu pricing techniques is called **contribution margin pricing**. This method is based on the exact cost of doing business, the amount of profit you want to earn, and the average number of customers you will serve. The total cost of doing business and the desired profit are divided by the average number of customers served.

Then the food cost for each item is added to the amount of money each guest must contribute to the business, and the menu price is set.

CONTRIBUTION MARGIN PRICING EXAMPLE	
Monthly cost of doing business	$25,000.00
Monthly profit	$ 5,000.00
Total monthly costs	$30,000.00
Average number of customers per month	2,000

$30,000.00 (total monthly cost) ÷ 2,000 (average customers) = $15.00

$15.00 is the amount each customer must spend to pay for the cost of doing business and to earn the desired profit. The cost of the food is added to the $15.00 to pay for the cost of the food.

CONTRIBUTION MARGIN PRICING MENU EXAMPLE

Menu Item A has a food cost of $4.55

Item A's menu price is $15.00 + $4.55 = $19.55

Item A's menu price is adjusted to $19.95

Menu Item B has a food cost of $3.65

Item B's menu price is $15.00 + $3.65 = $18.65

Item B's menu price is adjusted to $18.95

Contribution margin pricing ensures that a business is profitable because the cost of doing business and the profit per customer are built into the price of each menu item.

Alcoholic Beverages

Alcoholic beverages include liquor, wine, and beer. Alcoholic beverage sales are common in casual, upscale casual, and fine-dining restaurants. The profit earned from selling alcoholic beverages is a welcome addition to the profit earned from food sales. Alcoholic beverages are unique in many ways.

LIQUOR CLASSIFICATION

There are three classes of liquor sold in restaurants: **well**, **call**, and **premium**. The well brands are the least expensive and are sold most often. Call and premium brands are only sold when they are specifically asked for by the guest. The prices for call and premium brands are higher than the well brands, with premium brands being the most expensive drink sold in a restaurant.

ALCOHOLIC BEVERAGE SERVICE

There are two ways alcoholic beverages are measured and served. The first is by using a **computerized beverage control system**. Computerized beverage control systems are common in large hotels and beverage operations. These control systems pump well liquor to **liquor pouring guns** that are behind each bar. Every time an ounce of liquor is dispensed from the liquor pouring gun, the cash register rings up a sale. Such systems make it difficult for an employee to offer a guest a free drink and for the employee to steal money from the cash register.

The other way that alcoholic beverages are measured and poured is by hand. Even when a computerized beverage control system is used, call and premium brands are often poured by hand. Pouring by hand may result in the loss of product through spilling and makes it easier for a bartender to offer a customer a free drink.

ALCOHOLIC BEVERAGE COST

Liquor and wine are purchased in a 750-mL or in a liter container, both metric units of measure. All alcoholic beverages in the United States are sold in fluid ounces. Therefore, each bottle purchased is converted into fluid ounces to determine the cost per drink. A 750-mL bottle contains 25.4 fl. oz., while a liter bottle contains 33.8 fl. oz.

Liter bottles are used in computerized beverage control systems. They are turned upside down and placed in a pump system. Some liquor can spill when the bottles are attached to the pump, so the number of fluid ounces per liter used to determine the cost per ounce is 33, with the .8 of a fluid ounce considered to be lost due to spillage.

DETERMINING COST PER FLUID OUNCE FOR A COMPUTERIZED BEVERAGE CONTROL SYSTEM

The cost per fluid ounce is determined by the cost per liter bottle ÷ 33 fl. oz.

If a bottle of well vodka costs $7.95, the cost per fluid ounce is

$7.95 (cost per liter) ÷ 33 (fl. oz.) = $0.24 per ounce

The cost for one fluid ounce of vodka is $0.24.

When alcoholic beverages are measured and poured by hand, the allowances for spillage and free drinks are greater than with a computerized beverage control system. The number of fluid ounces per liter used in the calculation can be 32, and the number of fluid ounces per 750 mL can be 24. This reduction of the number of ounces per liter produces a more realistic beverage cost and beverage cost percent.

DETERMINING COST PER FLUID OUNCE FOR A HAND-POURED SYSTEM

The cost per fluid ounce is determined by the cost per liter bottle ÷ 32 fluid ounces.

If a bottle of well vodka costs $7.95, the cost per fluid ounce is:

$7.95 (cost per liter) ÷ 32 (fluid ounces) = $0.25

The cost for one fluid ounce of vodka is $0.25.

The cost per fluid ounce for the vodka in the preceding examples is within $0.01 of each other, with the computerized beverage control system having the lower cost. It is important to note that the volume of sales is much higher when a computerized beverage control system is used.

ALCOHOLIC BEVERAGE MENU PRICING

In the beverage industry the most common method for pricing an alcoholic beverage is called the **one-price method.** This method prices all well drinks at one price, all call drinks at one price, and all premium drinks at one price.

ONE-PRICE METHOD EXAMPLE	
Well drinks	$6.00
Call drinks	$8.00
Premium drinks	$12.00

The menu price of alcoholic beverages is in whole dollars to make it easier for the bartender and beverage server to give the customer change.

BEVERAGE COST PERCENT

A **beverage cost percent** is determined by using a beverage cost percent formula. This is the same as Formula III used to determine a food cost percent.

BEVERAGE COST PERCENT EXAMPLE
Cost of beverage ÷ Menu price × 100* = Beverage cost percent
A fluid ounce of well vodka costs $0.25.
The cost of the ice, the mix, and any garnish used in the drink is $0.10.
The total cost for the vodka and the ice, mix, and garnish is $0.35.
The one price for well drinks is $6.00
$0.35 (cost of vodka, ice, mix, garnish) ÷ $6.00 (price per well drink) = .06 × 100 = 6%
The beverage cost percent for well vodka is 6%.
*This changes the decimal to a percent.

The beverage cost percent is monitored to make sure it remains constant over time. If it does, then the operation is doing well. If the beverage cost percent fluctuates over time, there may be a problem that needs to be investigated.

Bakery and Pastry Industry Pricing

Pricing in the bakery and pastry industry is unique. The actual food cost for items that contain a large amount of low-cost ingredients, such as flour, sugar, and fat, is not a good indicator of the market value of these items. One important factor of pricing is the cost of the employees who have the specialized talent needed to produce a quality product. A professional baker and a creative cake decorator are paid higher salaries than others in this industry. Their salaries must be considered in the pricing of these items.

The one-price method is commonly used for items that are the same or similar. All breads are the same price per loaf. All large cookies are one price. All 8-inch round cakes are the same price, as well as all one-quarter sheet cakes, one-half sheet cakes, full sheet cakes, and so on. All fruit pies are the same price. All single specialty pastry items may also be priced the same.

Some bakery products, such as donuts, rolls, and bagels, are priced by the dozen. Some bakeries weigh items on scales in front of the customers and charge by the pound. The customer can purchase a certain number of cookies priced by the pound or a certain-sized coffee cake priced by the pound.

Then there are wedding cakes. Wedding cakes are priced anywhere from $100.00 to thousands of dollars. The price for a wedding cake depends on the reputation of the bakery, the size of the cake, and the amount and type of detail involved in the decoration. A bakery that specializes in wedding cakes can be a very profitable business.

The actual price charged per item, per dozen, or per cake depends on the cost of doing business for the bakery and the profit the owner wants to earn. The volume of business, the amount of labor involved in producing the item, and the cost of labor are other factors considered in determining the menu price for items in the bakery and pastry industry.

 ## Conclusion

Menu pricing plays a significant role in the success of the foodservice operation. Many factors impact this particular decision-making process. The cost of the food, the cost of employee talent, the other costs of doing business, and the amount of profit the business would like to earn are all key factors that need to be considered. Then there are different methods for pricing a menu and different pricing strategies for the different segments of the foodservice industry.

 ## Menu Pricing:
REVIEW PROBLEMS

1. Explain the following terms and their use in menu pricing:

a. À la carte pricing

b. Table d'hôte pricing

c. Prix fixe

d. One-price method

e. By the dozen

2. Food cost percent pricing: Fill in the blanks in the tables that follow.

Formula I: Food Cost ÷ Food Cost Percent = Menu Price

Food Cost	÷	Food Cost Percent	=	Menu Price
$2.50	÷	25%	=	
$2.50	÷	30%	=	
$2.50	÷	40%	=	
$4.18	÷	35%	=	
$5.39	÷	20%	=	
$8.11	÷	10%	=	
$8.57	÷	25%	=	
$9.29	÷	25%	=	
$12.22	÷	25%	=	
$12.79	÷	45%	=	

Formula II: Menu Price × Food Cost Percent = Food Cost

Menu Price	×	Food Cost Percent	=	Food Cost
$3.95	×	12%	=	
$6.95	×	10%	=	
$12.95	×	20%	=	
$15.95	×	30%	=	
$21.95	×	25%	=	
$40.00	×	40%	=	
$56.50	×	30%	=	
$80.00	×	20%	=	
$125.00	×	40%	=	
$200.00	×	38%	=	

Formula III: Food Cost ÷ Menu Price × 100 = Food Cost Percent

Food Cost	÷	Menu Price	×	100	=	Food Cost Percent
$2.24	÷	$9.95	×	100	=	
$0.96	÷	$7.95	×	100	=	
$4.44	÷	$24.95	×	100	=	
$3.12	÷	$15.95	×	100	=	
$5.26	÷	$28.95	×	100	=	
$1.89	÷	$9.95	×	100	=	
$3.00	÷	$12.95	×	100	=	
$2.67	÷	$7.95	×	100	=	
$13.62	÷	$65.00	×	100	=	
$22.38	÷	$125.00	×	100	=	

3. *Contribution margin pricing.* Price the menu based on the following information.

Weekly cost of doing business:	$4,000.00
Weekly profit:	$1,000.00
Total weekly cost:	$5,000.00
Average number of customers weekly:	4800

a. What amount is needed per customer to pay for the weekly cost of doing business and earning a profit?

b. Based on the following food costs, what is the menu price?

Item	Food Cost	+		=	Menu Price
A	$1.79	+		=	
B	$2.24	+		=	
C	$3.60	+		=	
D	$3.99	+		=	

4. In your opinion, which pricing method is better to use: food cost percent or contribution margin pricing, and why?

5. *Alcoholic beverage pricing.* The number of ounces per bottle is adjusted for spillage and free drinks to good customers.

a. If a 750-mL bottle of well liquor costs $9.50, what is the cost per ounce?

The cost for the ice, mix, and garnish is $0.15. The price per well drink is $5.00. What is the beverage cost percent?

b. If a liter bottle of call liquor costs $16.25 and is hand poured, what is the cost per ounce?

The cost for the ice, mix, and garnish is $0.20. The price per call drink is $8.00. What is the beverage cost percent?

Why is the pricing used in the beverage industry different than the pricing used in the sale of food?

Running Case Study

Step V

Thomas begins the process of developing menu prices for the three entrée items he will sell at *Tomas,* his Italian restaurant. He begins by considering the different pricing strategies and asking the following questions: Would his customers prefer à la carte, table d'hôte, or prix fixe pricing? Which strategy would yield a higher profit? Which strategy might bring customers back into the restaurant for additional meals?

Another consideration for Thomas is the side dishes he will offer to his customers. He has developed recipes and a cost per portion for his entrée items, but he needs to add additional items to his menu offerings. Thomas decides to experiment with two different menus. He begins with an à la carte menu and uses a 20% food cost percent to determine the menu prices.

Menu I: À la Carte Pricing

Entrées

The Best Meatballs Ever

Food Cost Per portion $1.17

Food Cost ÷ Food Cost Percent = Menu Price

$1.17 (cost per portion) ÷ .20 (20% food cost percent) = $5.85

Menu price adjusted to $5.95

Beef Braised in Red Wine
Food Cost Per Portion $1.82

Food Cost ÷ Food Cost Percent = Menu Price

$1.82 (cost per portion) ÷ .20 (20% food cost percent) = $9.10

Menu price adjusted to $9.95

Veal Scaloppine
Food Cost per Portion $1.69

Food Cost ÷ Food Cost Percent = Menu Price

$1.69 (cost per portion) ÷ .20 (20% food cost percent) = $8.45

Menu price adjusted to $8.95

Side Dishes

Pasta
Estimated Cost per Portion with Sauce $0.60

Food Cost ÷ Food Cost Percent = Menu Price

$0.60 (estimated cost per portion) ÷ .20 (20% food cost percent) = $3.00

Menu price adjusted to $3.95

Vegetable
Estimated Cost per Portion $0.80

Food Cost ÷ Food Cost Percent = Menu Price

$0.80 (estimated cost per portion) ÷ .20 (20% food cost percent) = $4.00

Menu price adjusted to $3.95

Salads

Dinner Salad
Estimated Cost per Portion $0.45

Food Cost ÷ Food Cost Percent = Menu Price

$0.45 (estimated food cost) ÷ .20 (20% food cost percent) = $2.25

Menu price left at $2.25

Antipasto Salad
Estimated Cost per Portion $1.85

Food Cost ÷ Food Cost Percent = Menu Price

$1.85 (estimated food cost) ÷ .20 (20% food cost percent) = $9.25

Menu price adjusted to ?*

*Thomas realizes this item's price needs to be lowered because a salad generally sells for less than the entrée prices.

Then, Thomas prices a table d'hôte menu. This menu includes a dinner salad, a side of pasta, and a vegetable with each entrée. The estimated cost of the dinner salad, side of pasta, and the vegetable are added together.

$0.45 (dinner salad) + $0.60 (side of pasta) + $0.80 (vegetable) = $1.85

The total cost for the table d'hôte items is $1.85.

This cost is added to each entrée item.

Menu II: Table d'Hôte Pricing

Entrée

Dinners include a salad, side of pasta, and a vegetable.

The Best Meatballs Ever

Food cost per portion $1.17 + $1.85 (items included with entrée) = $3.02

Food cost ÷ Food cost percent = Menu price

$3.02 (total cost per meal) ÷ .20 (20% food cost percent) = $15.10

Menu price adjusted to $15.95

Beef Braised in Red Wine

Food cost per portion $1.82 + $1.85 (items included with entrée) = $3.67

Food cost ÷ Food cost percent = Menu price

$3.67 (total cost per meal) ÷ .20 (20% food cost percent) = $18.35

Menu price adjusted to $18.95

Veal Scaloppine

Food cost per portion $1.69 + $1.85 (items included with entrée) = $3.54

Food cost ÷ Food cost percent = Menu price

$3.54 (total cost per meal) ÷ .20 (20% food cost percent) = $17.70

Menu price adjusted to $17.95

Thomas's menus are complete.

Answer the following questions based on the two menus Thomas has developed.

1. Are the side dishes offered complementary to the entrée offerings?

2. In your opinion, is a 20% food cost percent too high, too low, or just right?

3. As a restaurant customer, do you prefer an à la carte or a table d'hôte menu?

4. As a business owner, do you prefer an à la carte or a table d'hôte menu?

5. What is your opinion of Thomas's menu price adjustments?

6. What would you charge for the antipasto salad on the à la carte menu?

7. In your opinion, which menu should Thomas use in *Tomas*?

Now that you have completed these questions, it is your turn to develop two menus for the entrée items you have been working on throughout this course.

CHAPTER 12

Basic Accounting *for* Foodservice Operations

Also Known As The Impact of Menu Pricing on Success and Profit

> *"An entrepreneur has mathematical formula for success: Gauge overhead."*
>
> —MARK LALLEMAND, OWNER OF MYOVERHEAD.COM

The success or failure of a restaurant is provided in a **profit and loss** statement. This is an accounting document that records all of the sales and all of the expenses of a business during a specific period of time. These statements offer valuable information regarding a business's potential for success or the problems it may experience.

LEARNING OBJECTIVES

1. To become familiar with the format for a profit and loss statement
2. To identify the revenue and cost of sales for a restaurant
3. To define the operating expenses, capital expenses, and profit for a restaurant
4. To review the contribution margin menu pricing method

The following example of a profit and loss statement is for *Tomas*, the Italian restaurant developed in our running case study. Because *Tomas* is not an operating restaurant, this projected profit and loss statement is not based on actual operating results, but on **projected operating results**. Projected operating results are estimations of the sales and expenses for a restaurant to be opened in the future.

Tomas Italian Restaurant

Projected Profit and Loss Statement June 20XX		
	Dollars	**Percentage**
Sales Revenue		
Food	$40,000.00	80%
Beverage	$10,000.00	20%
Total Revenue	$50,000.00	100%
Cost of Sales		
Cost of Food	$ 8,000.00	20% of $40,000 (food cost)
Cost of Beverage	$ 1,500.00	15% of $10,000 (beverage cost)
Total Cost of Sales	$ 9,500.00	
[$50,000.00 (total revenue) − $9,500.00 (total cost) = $40,500.00]		
Gross Profit	$40,500.00	
Operating Expenses		
Salaries and Wages	$12,000.00	24% of $50,000 (direct labor cost)
Employee Benefits	$ 3,000.00	6% of $50,000 (benefit cost)
China, Glassware, Flatware, Linens	$ 50.00	
Cleaning Supplies	$ 295.00	
Uniforms	$ 525.00	
Menus	$ 0.00	
Paper Products	$ 400.00	
Administrative and General	$ 255.00	
Marketing and Advertising	$ 50.00	
Operations and Maintenance	$ 325.00	
Utilities	$ 1,200.00	
Total Operating Expenses	$18,100.00	
[$40,500.00 (gross profit) − $18,100.00 (total operating expenses) = $22,400.00]		
Income Before Capital Expenses	$22,400.00	
Capital Expenses		
Insurance	$ 750.00	
Rent	$ 4,000.00	
Real Estate Taxes	$ 800.00	
Interest Expense	$ 1,450.00	
Depreciation	$ 2,900.00	
Total Capital Expenses	$ 9,900.00	
[$22,400.00 (income before capital expenses) − $9,900.00 (capital expenses) = $12,500.00]		
Profit Before Income Taxes	$12,500.00	

By estimating the revenue and the expenses using the profit and loss format, a business has the ability to determine if it has the potential to earn a profit. If the projected operating results indicate potential problems, the numbers can be adjusted, or changed, in the projections to ensure a successful operation. The key to success is to translate the projected operating results into a business that can earn a profit.

The format of this projected profit and loss statement, as well as the revenue and expense account names, are the standards used in the foodservice industry. The previous projected profit and loss statement for *Tomas* is presented in this standardized format.

Sales Revenue and Cost of Sales

The projected profit and loss statement for *Tomas* anticipates $40,000.00 in food sales and $10,000.00 in beverage sales. The total sales revenue for the month of June 20XX is $50,000.00. In Chapter 11 on menu pricing, Thomas decided to price his menu with a food cost percent of 20%. Using Formula II (see page 140), the total projected cost of food for the month is 20% of $40,000.00, which equals $8,000.00.

> $40,000.00 × 20% (.20 as a decimal) = $8,000.00

Thomas is projecting a 15% beverage cost percent, because he believes alcoholic beverage sales will come primarily from wine, which has a higher beverage cost than liquor. The total beverage sales for the month are predicted to be $10,000.00. Using Formula II, the total cost for beverage is 15% of $10,000.00, or $1,500.00.

> $10,000.00 × 15% (.15 as a decimal) = $1,500.00

Food cost and beverage cost are the **cost of sales** in the foodservice industry. The accuracy of the revenue projections for food and beverage sales is critical to determining whether or not this business operation will be a successful one. Not only does the revenue have to pay for all of the other expenses listed on the projected profit and loss statement, but there should also be money left for the profit Thomas is hoping to earn.

It is common for a new business to overestimate the amount of revenue it will earn. This overestimation is the cause of many business failures. It is also common for a new business to underestimate the costs of doing business, for example, the cost of food used in the month of June 20XX.

Remember, Thomas priced his menu in Chapter 11, "Menu Pricing," using a predetermined food cost percent of 20%, but it is very likely the actual food cost percent for a new restaurant will be higher than the predetermined cost. This means the cost of food for the month of June 20XX will probably be higher than the $8,000.00 projected on the profit and loss statement.

Operating Expenses, Capital Expenses, and Profit

Operating expenses are the costs of doing business which may vary month to month. Some of these expenses are small, while others need to be monitored to ensure a profit. The operating expense with the highest cost is the cost of employees.

The combined cost of salaries, wages, and employee benefits is projected to be $15,000.00 for the month of June 20XX at *Tomas*. This is higher than the projected cost of the food and beverage. A full 30% of the $50,000.00 in sales revenue is needed to cover these employee costs.

$$\$15,000.00 \div \$50,000.00 = .30 \text{ or } 30\%$$

This is one area that management must watch carefully.

The other area on which management must keep a watchful eye is the cost of utilities. The restaurant business is an energy-intensive business. The equipment used to store and prepare food is run by electricity or natural gas. The cost of electricity and natural gas has been increasing, and it is going to continue to do so. As the cost of energy increases, the profit for the restaurant decreases. An energy control program can help to keep energy costs in line with cost projections.

Capital expenses include rent, insurance, and real estate taxes. These are determined by the landlord, an insurance company, and the local government. This cost category needs careful consideration before the business opens, because capital expenses must be paid regardless of the revenue the business generates.

The goal of every **for-profit** business is to make money. The money the business earns is called the **profit**. The profit is determined by subtracting all of the costs associated with running the business from the total sales revenue. Some businesses make a profit, and some businesses do not.

The projected profit and loss statement for *Tomas* lists the profit before income taxes as $12,500.00 for June of 20XX. Every expense that exceeds the costs listed on the profit and loss statement takes money away from the projected profit. If, for example, the cost of food is $9,000.00 instead of $8,000.00, the profit decreases by $1,000.00. If the food cost increases by $1,000.00, the profit becomes $11,500.00.

Contribution Margin Menu Pricing

Contribution margin menu pricing was discussed in Chapter 11. This menu pricing method adds all of the costs of doing business to the desired profit and divides the sum by the number of customers served to calculate a base menu price.

The cost of the food is then added to this base. This method ensures the costs of doing business and the profit are covered equally by each customer served in the restaurant.

Thomas is going to use the information contained in the projected profit and loss statement to calculate a base menu price for *Tomas*. First, Thomas adds the total cost of the operating expenses to the total cost of the capital expenses. Then Thomas adds the projected profit to the sum.

Total operating expenses:	$18,100.00
Total capital expenses:	$ 9,900.00
Total costs	$28,000.00
Plus the profit	$12,500.00
Total costs and profit	$40,500.00

The $40,500.00 plus the cost of food is the total amount of money Thomas needs his customers to spend to cover his costs and to make his profit. If Thomas serves 2,000 customers in June of 20XX, the base menu price is as follows:

$40,500.00 (costs and profit) ÷ 2,000 (number of customers) = $20.25

Contribution menu pricing shows Thomas that his base menu price is $20.25 in order for him to cover his costs and to earn a profit. Thomas must now add the cost of his food to this $20.25. Let's compare this pricing method to the food cost percent method used in Chapter 11.

MENU I: À LA CARTE PRICING

Entrées

The Best Meatballs Ever

Food cost per portion $1.17

Food cost ÷ Food cost percent = Menu price

$1.17 (food cost per portion) ÷ .20 (20% food cost percent) = $5.85

Menu price adjusted to $5.95

Food cost percent pricing yields a menu price of $5.95 for the Best Meatballs Ever.

Contribution margin pricing yields a menu price of $21.95 for the Best Meatballs Ever.

$20.25 (base price) + $1.17 (food cost per portion) = $21.42

Menu price adjusted to $21.95

The difference between the contribution margin menu price and the food cost percent menu price is $16.00.

$21.95 (contribution margin price) − $5.95 (food cost price) = $16.00

Beef Braised in Red Wine

Food cost per portion $1.82

Food cost ÷ Food cost percent = Menu price

$1.82 (food cost per portion) ÷ .20 (20% food cost percent) = $9.10

Menu price adjusted to $9.95

Food cost percent pricing yields a menu price of $9.95 for Beef Braised in Red Wine.

Contribution margin pricing yields a menu price of $22.95 for Beef Braised in Red Wine.

$20.25 (base price) + $1.82 (food cost per portion) = $22.07

Menu price adjusted to $22.95

The difference between the contribution margin menu price and the food cost percent menu price is $13.00.

$22.95 (contribution margin price) − $9.95 (food cost price) = $13.00

Veal Scalloppine

Food cost per portion $1.69

Food cost ÷ Food cost percent = Menu price

$1.69 (food cost per portion) ÷ .20 (20% food cost percent) = $8.45

Menu price adjusted to $8.95

Food cost percent pricing yields a menu price of $8.95 for Veal Scaloppine.

Contribution margin pricing yields a menu price of $21.95 for Veal Scaloppine.

$20.25 (base price) + $1.69 (food cost per portion) = $21.94

Menu price adjusted to $21.95

The difference between the contribution margin menu price and the food cost percent menu price is $13.00.

$21.95 (contribution margin price) − $8.95 (food cost price) = $13.00

As Thomas looks at the difference in menu prices based on food cost percent pricing and contribution margin pricing for the three entrée items he plans on serving at *Tomas*, he begins to realize that he needs to reevaluate his menu prices. Thomas decides to skip over the side dishes from the à la carte menu and to recalculate the table d'hôte menu prices using the contribution margin price of $20.25.

The table d'hôte menu includes a dinner salad, a side of pasta, and a vegetable with each entrée. The estimated cost of the dinner salad, side of pasta, and the vegetable are added together.

$0.45 (dinner salad) + $0.60 (side of pasta) + $0.80 (vegetable) = $1.85

The total cost for the table d'hôte items is $1.85.

This cost is added to each entrée item.

MENU II: TABLE D'HÔTE PRICING

Entrée

Dinners include a salad, side of pasta, and a vegetable.

The Best Meatballs Ever

Food cost per portion $1.17 + $1.85 (items included with entrée) = $3.02

Food cost ÷ Food cost percent = Menu price

$3.02 (total cost per meal) ÷ .20(20% food cost percent) = $15.10

Menu price adjusted to $15.95

Food cost percent pricing yields a menu price of $15.95 for the Best Meatballs Ever meal.

Contribution margin pricing yields a menu price of $23.95 for the Best Meatballs Ever meal.

$20.25 (base price) = $3.02 (total cost per meal) = $23.27

Menu price adjusted to $23.95

The difference between the contribution margin menu price and the food cost percent menu price is $8.00.

$23.95 (contribution margin price) − $15.95 (food cost percent price) = $8.00

Beef Braised in Red Wine

Food cost per portion $1.82 + $1.85 (items included with entrée) = $3.67

Food cost ÷ Food cost percent = Menu price

$3.67 (total cost per meal) ÷ .20 (20% food cost percent) = $18.35

Menu price adjusted to $18.95

Food cost percent pricing yields a menu price of $18.95 for Beef Braised in Red Wine.

Contribution margin pricing yields a menu price of $23.95 for Beef Braised in Red Wine.

$20.25 (base price) + $3.67 (total cost per meal) = $23.92

Menu price adjusted to $23.95

The difference between the contribution margin menu price and the food cost percent menu price is $5.00.

$23.95 (contribution margin price) − $18.95 (food cost percent price) = $5.00

Veal Scaloppine

Food cost per portion $1.69 + $1.85 (items included with entrée) = $3.54

Food cost ÷ Food cost percent = Menu price

$3.54 (total cost per meal) ÷ .20 (20% food cost percent) = $17.70

Menu price adjusted to $17.95

Food cost percent pricing yields a menu price of $17.95 for Veal Scaloppine.

Contribution margin pricing yields a menu price of $23.95 for Veal Scaloppine.

$20.25 (base price) + $3.54 (total cost per meal) = $23.79

Menu price adjusted to $23.95

The difference between the contribution margin menu price and the food cost percent price is $6.00

$23.95 (contribution margin price) − $17.95 (food cost percent price) = $6.00

Thomas places the two menu pricing methods side by side in the à la carte menu format and the table d'hôte menu format.

MENU I: À LA CARTE PRICING	
Food Cost Percent Price	Contribution Margin Price
The Best Meatballs Ever	
$5.95	$21.95
Beef Braised in Red Wine	
$9.95	$22.95
Veal Scaloppine	
$8.95	$21.95

MENU II: TABLE D'HÔTE	
The Best Meatballs Ever	
$15.95	$23.95
Beef Braised in Red Wine	
$18.95	$23.95
Veal Scaloppine	
$17.95	$23.95

Thomas notices that the price differences between the food cost percent pricing method and the contribution margin pricing method are smaller for the table d'hôte menu than for the à la carte menu prices. He realizes that if he uses the à la carte menu option, the guests will hopefully be purchasing other menu items. If this happens, the $20.25 base price can be shared by the entrée items and the side dishes.

Thomas also realizes that the individual menu price for all of the meals on the table d'hôte menu is $23.95. The reason is that the cost of the food for each of the three entrées is within $0.65 of each other. The small difference in the food cost produces the same menu price once the prices are adjusted after the calculations. This gives Thomas another menu pricing idea. Should he have a prix fixe menu, where every entrée sells for the same price? The fixed price at *Tomas* would be $23.95.

 ## Conclusion

A profit and loss statement is an industry standard used to evaluate the success or failure of a business. A projected profit and loss statement is a tool that can be used to evaluate a new business's potential for profit and success. It can be used to determine if some of the revenues are too optimistic or if some costs are too low.

A projected profit and loss statement can also be used to develop contribution margin menu prices. The contribution margin menu pricing method is not only a useful way to determine menu prices, but this method also helps to ensure that the costs of doing business and the profit are covered equally by each customer served in the restaurant.

 ## Basic Accounting for Foodservice Operations: REVIEW PROBLEMS

1. *Menu pricing.* Thomas has calculated new menu prices using the projected profit and loss statement and the contribution margin menu pricing method. He has developed four menu pricing options:

The original à la carte menu

The original table d'hôte menu

The contribution margin à la carte menu

The contribution margin table d'hôte menu, which is a prix fixe menu.

2. What are the advantages of each of these pricing options?

   a. The original à la carte menu

   b. The original table d'hôte menu

   c. The contribution margin à la carte menu

   d. The contribution margin table d'hôte menu, which is a prix fixe menu

3. What are the disadvantages of each of these pricing methods?

   a. The original à la carte menu

   b. The original table d'hôte menu

   c. The contribution margin à la carte menu

   d. The contribution margin table d'hôte menu, which is a prix fixe menu

4. Which of these four options do you feel Thomas should use in his restaurant, *Tomas*? Please explain.

5. Profit and loss statement review. Refer to the projected profit and loss statement in this chapter or in Appendix V. What is the impact on profit if the following changes in revenue or costs occur?

   a. The food cost percent increases to 22% of sales.

   b. The beverage cost percent decreases to 12% of sales.

   c. The sales revenue increases by 10%.

   d. The sales revenue decreases by 10%.

   e. The cost for employee salaries and wages increases by 12%.

   f. The cost of employee benefits increases by 20%.

g. The cost of utilities increases by 3%.

h. Thomas places an order for new menus. The cost is $2,500.00.

i. The landlord has decided to increase the rent by $1,000.00 per month.

6. *Contribution margin menu pricing.* Calculate the base menu price for the following scenarios.

Scenario A

Total operating expenses:	$16,500.00
Total capital expenses:	$8,900.00
Total costs	$
Plus the profit	$10,000.00
Total costs and profit	$

Total number of customers: 1,200.

Base menu price is:

Scenario B

Total operating expenses:	$21,300.00
Total capital expenses:	$13,000.00
Total costs	$
Plus the profit	$15,500.00
Total costs and profit	$

Total number of customers: 2,500.

Base menu price is:

Scenario C

Total operating expenses:	$14,250.00
Total capital expenses:	$7,000.00
Total costs	$
Plus the profit	$8,000.00
Total costs and profit	$

Total number of customers: 1,400.

Base menu price is:

Scenario D

Total operating expenses:	$10,000.00
Total capital expenses:	$6,500.00
Total costs	$
Plus the profit	$15,000.00
Total costs and profit	$

Total number of customers: 800.

Base menu price is:

Running Case Study

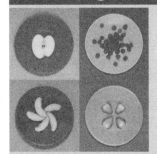

Step VI—Profit and Loss Statements

The projected profit and loss statement for *Tomas*, the case study restaurant, appears in this chapter. Appendix V contains a copy of *Tomas's* profit and loss statement, as well as a blank profit and loss statement.

Your assignment is to complete the blank profit and loss statement using information concerning the cost of running a restaurant from your local area. You can contact a local restaurateur, the chamber of commerce, a commercial realtor, or anyone who can assist you to develop the estimated costs of running a restaurant.

You can then determine the amount of profit you would like to earn. The food cost percent used for your menu prices in Chapter 11 is the cost percent you should use. After the profit and loss statement is complete, estimate the number of customers you will serve. With this information, reprice your menu entrées using the contribution margin pricing method.

CHAPTER **13**

Labor Cost *and* Control Techniques

"You cannot run a restaurant without employees, but it would be more profitable if you could."

—TERRI JONES

As the projected profit and loss statement for *Tomas* in Chapter 12 pointed out, the cost of labor is the highest operating expense for a typical foodservice operation. Labor cost can average 30 to 35 percent of sales. In some operations, labor costs can be as high as 40 percent of sales. This means that for every dollar we collect in food sales, $0.30 to $0.35 or perhaps even $0.40 is spent to cover the cost of labor. The formula for labor cost percent is as follows:

> Labor cost percent = Cost of labor ÷ Total sales revenue

The projected labor cost percent for *Tomas,* as listed on the projected profit and loss statement, including employee benefits is 30%.

> Labor cost percent for *Tomas* = $15,000.00 ÷ $50,000.00 = .30 or 30%

LEARNING OBJECTIVES

1. To understand the governments' role in payroll administration
2. To identify the cost associated with hiring employees

3. To realize the impact organized labor has on labor costs

4. To comprehend the value of a staffing guide

5. To understand the importance of a forecast of customer counts

6. To utilize the forecast of customer counts to prepare weekly employee work schedules

7. To calculate employee payroll

 ## The Cost of Labor

The actual dollar amount paid to an employee is only the beginning of our labor costs. In many foodservice operations, employees are offered benefits. **Benefits** can include health, dental, and vision insurance; paid vacation; sick and bereavement leave; or even a retirement plan. The cost of these benefits is an additional expense to the employer. Then, there are taxes.

The burden of tax collection and payment falls to the employer, who in this case, is the foodservice company. There is the cost associated with the mechanics of payroll and the disbursement of monies to the various governmental taxing agencies. The employer is liable for 50% of an employee's Social Security tax (FICA), and the entire federal (FUTA) and state (SUTA) tax for unemployment and injured worker's compensation. The employer is also liable to pay these taxes for monies earned as tips by food and beverage servers and bartenders.

The wise foodservice operator uses several techniques to ensure that the operation is properly staffed to meet the needs of the customers and payroll costs are kept at a certain percentage of sales. The ability to control labor costs depends on many factors. The greatest influence on labor cost is organized labor. **Organized labor** means that the employees are represented by and are members of a union.

Culinary union membership is highest in large metropolitan areas in the United States. Las Vegas, Nevada; Miami, Florida; New York City, New York; and San Francisco, California are examples of large metropolitan areas in the United States with large culinary union membership.

There are many advantages for members of a labor union. Generally speaking, union members earn a higher hourly wage and have a better benefit package than nonunion workers. Another advantage of union membership is an "almost" guarantee of a 40-hour workweek.

Union membership increases the cost of labor for the foodservice operator. Union rules can make it difficult or even impossible for a foodservice operator to practice some labor-control techniques. Therefore, it is crucial for both union and a nonunion operation to hire and schedule employees properly. Proper hiring and scheduling begins with a staffing guide.

Staffing Guide

A **staffing guide** is a chart or graph that indicates the number of employees needed based on the forecasted number of customers per hour. The chart or graph begins with zero customers and ends with the maximum number of customers that can be seated in the dining room at one time. The staffing guide balances zero customers with a "skeleton" staff who prepare the operation for the arrival of the customers and a "skeleton" staff who clean the operation at the end of the day.

Employee scheduling is then based on the forecasted number of customers. There is a separate staffing guide for each job category. Job categories might include cashier, host/hostess, food server, beverage server, bartender, sous-chef, line cook, dishwasher, and so on.

 # Labor Cost Control for *Tomas*

At *Tomas*, Thomas anticipates having 100 seats in his dining room. The average food server can serve 25 customers per hour. The maximum number of food servers who can work in the dining room is 4. One food server will come in before the restaurant is open to prepare the service area. This server would ice the soft-drink machine; start the coffee; check the sugar, salt, and pepper; and so on.

STAFFING GUIDE: DINING ROOM SERVERS FOR *TOMAS*	
Staffing Guide for Food Servers	
Number of Customers	Number of Food Servers
0	1
1 to 25	1
26 to 50	2
51 to 75	3
76 to 100	4

Thomas anticipates that each line cook will prepare food for up to 20 customers per hour. The maximum number of cooks who can work behind the line is five. Thomas would schedule two line cooks to come in before the restaurant opens in order to complete all of the necessary preparation.

STAFFING GUIDE: LINE COOKS FOR *TOMAS*	
Staffing Guide for Line Cooks	
Number of Customers	Number of Line Cooks
0	2
1 to 40	2
41 to 60	3
61 to 80	4
More than 81	5

The staffing guide assists with the scheduling of employees based on the needs of the customers. It assists with labor cost control because customer demand dictates employee schedules.

 # Employee Schedules for *Tomas*

The first step to employee scheduling is to forecast the number of customers who will visit the restaurant per meal period. *Tomas* will be open for dinner seven nights a week from 4 PM to 10 PM. Employees will need to be scheduled before opening for preparation and after closing for cleanup.

Thomas forecasts the number of customers who will visit each hour of the dinner meal period. Remember, in Chapter 12 Thomas predicted he would serve 2,000 customers per month or 500 customers per week. The following forecast of customer counts anticipates 500 customers each week.

Thomas realizes that a new restaurant will not be busy until it has proven itself to its potential customer base. This is the justification for the forecast of customer counts per hour. Thomas now looks at the number of food servers and

Forecast of Customer Counts per Hour for *Tomas*

Hours	Sunday	Monday	Tuesday	Wednesday	Thursday	Friday	Saturday
3 to 4	0	0	0	0	0	0	0
4 to 5	5	5	5	5	8	8	10
5 to 6	10	5	5	12	15	20	25
6 to 7	10	15	15	20	20	30	30
7 to 8	10	10	8	20	20	30	30
8 to 9	10	5	5	10	10	20	20
9 to 10	2	2	2	2	2	2	2
10 to 11	0	0	0	0	0	0	0

Number of Food Servers Needed Based on Customer Counts per Hour for *Tomas*

Hours	Sunday	Monday	Tuesday	Wednesday	Thursday	Friday	Saturday
3 to 4	1	1	1	1	1	1	1
4 to 5	1	1	1	1	1	1	1
5 to 6	1	1	1	1	1	1	1
6 to 7	1	1	1	1	1	2	2
7 to 8	1	1	1	1	1	2	2
8 to 9	1	1	1	1	1	1	1
9 to 10	1	1	1	1	1	1	1
10 to 11	1	1	1	1	1	1	1

line cooks he needs to schedule based on the staffing guide and the anticipated customer counts per hour.

Based on the staffing guide for food servers, Thomas needs 1 food server for every 25 customers per hour. Thomas develops a schedule with the number of servers needed for each day and hour of the week.

Because Thomas only anticipates more than 25 customers per hour on Friday and Saturday between 6 and 8, he determines he only needs to have 1 food server in the dining room between 6 and 8 except for Friday and Saturday. The total amount of hours for which a food server is needed is as follows:

> 7 (days a week) × 8 (hours per day) = 56 hours per week for a food server
>
> *plus*
>
> 2 hours on Friday and 2 hours on Saturday evenings where customer counts exceed 25 customers per hour.
>
> Thomas needs food servers to work a total of 60 hours a week.

Thomas realizes he needs to hire at least 2 food servers. He ponders the following questions:

1. Should I hire a full-time food server?
2. If I hire a full-time food server, will I need to offer benefits?
3. Should I hire only part-time food servers?
4. If I hire only part-time food servers, will they have the same commitment to the customers as a full-time employee?
5. Will part-time food servers leave for a full-time position elsewhere?
6. Does state law require an employee to work a minimum of a 4 hour shift?

Schedule: Dining Room Servers

Servers	Sunday	Monday	Tuesday	Wednesday	Thursday	Friday	Saturday
Mikayla	Off	Off	3 to 11	3 to 11	3 to 11	3 to 11	3 to 11
Kayli	3 to 11	3 to 11	Off	Off	Off	5:30 – 9:30	5:30 – 9:30

Thomas decides to hire one full-time and one part-time food server. The full-time food server will work 5 days a week and the part-time food server will work four days a week. The anticipated schedule for the food servers is shown above. The total number of hours for food servers is actually 64 hours, not 60 as Thomas had calculated. This is because state laws do require that an employee have a minimum of 4 hours per shift.

Mikayla is a full-time food server and is scheduled to work 40 hours per week. She is eligible for benefits because she works full-time. Kayli is a part-time food server who is scheduled to work 24 hours per week. She is not eligible for benefits because she works part-time. Both Mikayla and Kayli are employees who earn tips in addition to their hourly wage.

Thomas now repeats this process for the line cooks. The minimum number of line cooks needed based on the staffing guide is 2 for up to 40 customers per hour. The forecast of Customer Counts per Hour for *Tomas* never exceeds 30 customers per hour. Therefore, 2 line cooks are scheduled 8 hours per day for 7 days a week.

The total number of hours the line cooks are needed is as follows:

7 (days per week) × 8 (hours per day) × 2 (number of line cooks) = 112 hours
Thomas needs line cooks to work 112 hours per week.

Number of Line Cooks Needed Based on Forecast of Customer Counts per Hour for *Tomas*

Hours	Sunday	Monday	Tuesday	Wednesday	Thursday	Friday	Saturday
3 to 4	2	2	2	2	2	2	2
4 to 5	2	2	2	2	2	2	2
5 to 6	2	2	2	2	2	2	2
6 to 7	2	2	2	2	2	2	2
7 to 8	2	2	2	2	2	2	2
8 to 9	2	2	2	2	2	2	2
9 to 10	2	2	2	2	2	2	2
10 to 11	2	2	2	2	2	2	2

Schedule: Line Cooks

Line Cooks	Sunday	Monday	Tuesday	Wednesday	Thursday	Friday	Saturday
Thomas	3 to 11	3 to 11	3 to 11	3 to 5	3 to 5	3 to 5	3 to 5
Ray	3 to 11	Off	Off	3 to 11	3 to 11	3 to 11	3 to 11
Dustin	Off	Off	Off	5 to 10	5 to 10	5 to 10	5 to 10

Thomas begins to consider the number of line cooks he needs to hire. If line cooks work 112 hours per week, he should hire at least 3 line cooks. Thomas knows he will be in the kitchen working along with the line cooks, so he begins to ponder the following questions:

1. If I work in the kitchen before opening, can I reduce the number of hours the line cooks work?

2. If I work in the kitchen on the slower nights, could I reduce the number of hours the line cooks work?

3. If I work in the kitchen, could I hire one full-time and one part-time line cook?

Thomas decides to work in the kitchen before opening and on the slower nights to eliminate the cost of one line cook. The schedule for line cooks is shown above.

Ray is a full-time line cook who works 40 hours a week and is eligible for benefits. Dustin is a part-time line cook who works 20 hours a week and is not eligible for benefits. Thomas schedules himself to work on the slower nights and to help Ray when Dustin is not working.

Thomas is always available to help the line cooks, and the food servers, if needed. Thomas saves the cost of one full-time line cook by placing himself on the schedule. Thomas hopes that as business increases, he will be able to hire another line cook.

Employee Payroll Calculations

Employees are paid for the hours they work. The basic payroll calculation is as follows:

$$\text{Number of hours worked} \times \text{Hourly pay rate} = \text{Gross pay}$$

Then the employer subtracts income tax (federal, state, and local), and Social Security tax from the employees' gross pay to arrive at the employees' net pay.

Raymond, the line cook who works full time, earns $15.00 an hour. If Raymond works 40 hours a week, what is his gross pay?

> 40 (number of hours worked) × $15.00 (hourly pay rate) = $600.00 gross pay

Raymond must pay federal and possibly state and local income taxes. For this example, federal, state, and local taxes are 18% (.18) of Raymond's gross income.

> $600.00 (gross pay) × .18 (18% of gross) = $108.00 amount of total income taxes

Raymond must also pay 7.5 percent (.075) of his gross wages for Social Security. Raymond's Social Security deduction is as follows:

> $600.00 (gross pay) × .075 (7.5% of gross) = $45.00 amount of Social Security deduction

Therefore, Raymond's gross income is reduced by $108.00 (income tax) and $45.00 (Social Security). What is his net pay?

> $600.00 − ($108.00 + $45.00) = $600.00 − $153.00 = $447.00 net pay

Raymond's net pay is $447.00.

Thomas is responsible to pay the federal, state, and local governments the monies withheld from Raymond's paycheck. There are also additional expenses Thomas must pay as Raymond's employer.

1. The total tax amount of $108.00: to the various taxation agencies, IRS, and so on.
2. The Social Security amount of $45.00 to the federal government
3. The 7.5% (.075) the employer pays to the federal government's fund for Raymond's Social Security. The cost to Thomas is $45.00. This is paid to the federal government.
4. The percentage of Raymond's gross pay to the federal FUTA and state SUTA government funds that cover an employee's unemployment and injured worker's compensation. For this example, the federal and state funds are 1%, respectively. The cost to Thomas is $600.00 × .01 (1%) = $6.00 to FUTA and $6.00 to SUTA. The total is $12.00.
5. Raymond is a benefit-eligible employee because he works full-time. The benefits Raymond receives cost Thomas an additional $3.00 for every hour that Raymond works.

This $3.00 per hour is paid to the health insurance company that provides coverage to the employees at *Tomas*. The cost to Thomas for Raymond's health insurance is $120.00 per week.

> 40 (number of hours Raymond worked) × $3.00 (amount per hour) = $120.00 for health insurance

Raymond's payroll is now complete.

	Gross Pay	Federal/State/ Local Taxes	Social Security	FUTA/ SUTA	Benefits
Raymond earns	$600.00				
Raymond pays to					
government		$108.00	$45.00		
Thomas pays to					
government for Raymond			$45.00	$12.00	
Thomas pays for					
Raymond's benefits					$120.00
Total cost to Thomas					
for Raymond	$600.00		$45.00	$12.00	$120.00
Total Thomas sends					
to governmental agencies		$108.00	$90.00	$12.00	

> Total cost to Thomas per week for Raymond, the full-time line cook:
>
> Raymond's gross pay: $600.00
> Thomas' share of Social Security: $45.00
> Thomas' cost for FUTA and SUTA: $12.00
> Thomas' cost for insurance: $120.00
> _____
> Total cost to Thomas for Raymond each week: $777.00
>
> The actual cost per hour for Raymond is not $15.00 per hour, but:
>
> $777.00 (Raymond's total cost) ÷ 40 (hours per week) = $19.43.

Thomas pays Raymond $15.00 per hour. The cost of Social Security, FUTA, SUTA, and benefits add an additional $4.43 to Raymond's hourly cost to Thomas.

> $19.43 (total cost per hour) − $15.00 (hourly wage) = $4.43

Through these calculations, Thomas realizes that the hourly pay rate of an employee is not the entire cost of the employee to the business. Thomas now focuses on the food servers who are tip earners.

Tip Earners

The Internal Revenue Service (IRS) has developed a system of taxation for employees who earn tips. Food servers, beverage servers, and bartenders are included as part of this system. The legislation is called the Tip Rate Determination Agreement (TRDA) or Tip Rate Alternative Commitment (TRAC). The TRDA or TRAC are basically agreements made by a foodservice operation with the IRS where employees earn tips. The agreement states that each tipped employee earns a certain dollar amount of tips per hour worked. The total of the hourly wage and the tip income is then used to determine the employee's and the employer's tax liability.

At *Tomas* the projected TRDA states that all of the food servers earn $7.50 an hour in tips. Thomas pays his food servers $4.25 per hour. This is less than the minimum wage. In some states it is legal to pay a tip earner less than the minimum wage because their tip income is considered part of their hourly pay. In other states, tip earners must be paid the minimum wage.

The TRDA complicates the paycheck process for Thomas as he calculates the paycheck for each of his food servers. For example, Mikayla, a food server, worked 40 hours last week:

> 40 (number of hours worked) × $4.25 (hourly pay rate) = $170.00 gross pay

However, Mikayla's federal, state, and local taxes, along with the Social Security payment and the FUTA and SUTA, are based on the $4.25 hourly rate plus the $7.50 an hour she earned as tipped income.

> $4.25 (hourly rate) + $7.50 (TRDA hourly rate) = $11.75 per TRDA hour

Mikayla's federal, state, and local taxes, along with her Social Security payment and the FUTA and SUTA are based on $11.75 an hour rather than her wage of $4.25 an hour:

> 40 (number of hours worked) × $11.75 (TRDA hourly rate) = $470.00 TRDA gross pay

Thomas pays Social Security and FUTA and SUTA for Mikayla based on a $470.00 paycheck.

Tomas is paying taxes on money his customers are giving to his employee as a gratuity for the quality of service she provided to them. Thomas never considered these additional expenses as he planned the financials for *Tomas*.

Thomas now has a better understanding of the total cost of having employees. He realizes why employee costs are the highest operating expense for a foodservice operation. He also recognizes the importance of labor cost control.

 ## Conclusion

The hourly rate employees are paid is a percentage of the total cost to the foodservice operator. The cost of labor can be the largest controllable expense of a foodservice operation. For this reason, the wise operator prepares a staffing guide and a weekly forecast of customer counts before scheduling employees. This ensures that customers will be served efficiently and payroll will be controlled.

 ## Labor Cost and Control Techniques: REVIEW PROBLEMS

1. Why is it important to control the cost of labor?

2. What is a staffing guide?

3. What are the advantages to utilizing a staffing guide?

4. What is a forecast of customer counts?

5. What is an employee schedule?

6. What are the advantages of forecasting prior to preparing the weekly employee schedule?

7. What is the basic formula for determining an employee's weekly pay?

8. What other components are included in the payroll calculations for employees?

9. Do employees actually earn more or less than their stated hourly wage? Why?

10. Using the following information, create a staffing guide and a schedule for the dishwashers at a local university's student cafeteria.

Staffing Guide and Schedule:

The cafeteria is open from 6 A.M. to 10 A.M. for breakfast, seven days a week. Five hundred students are eligible to eat in the cafeteria, but the average number of students for breakfast is 250. The average customer counts are as follows:

6 to 7 A.M.	25 students
7 to 8 A.M.	75 students
8 to 9 A.M.	100 students
9 to 10 A.M.	50 students

The dishwashers wash both the pots and pans used for food prep and the serving dishes. The cafeteria needs 1 dishwasher per hour for every 25 students. The minimum shift is 2 hours.

Staffing Guide: Dishwashers

Number of Students	Number of Dishwashers

Schedule: Dishwashers

Sunday	Monday	Tuesday	Wednesday	Thursday	Friday	Saturday

11. Payroll calculations. Mikayla is a waitress who will work at *Tomas*. She will work 40 hours a week and earns $4.25 an hour and will have a TRDA of $7.50 an hour.

a. What will Mikayla's gross pay be per paycheck?

b. If the combined federal, state, and local tax rate is 21%, what is Mikayla's tax liability?

c. Social Security is taxed at a rate of 7.5% for the employee and the employer. What is the Social Security tax on Mikayla's earnings? Remember, both Mikayla and Thomas contribute 7.5% to Mikayla's Social Security account.

d. What is Mikayla's net income?

e. Thomas pays FUTA and SUTA for Mikayla at a rate of 1.5% for each fund. What is the total cost of FUTA and SUTA to *Tomas*?

f. Mikayla is a full-time employee and is eligible for benefits. Thomas pays $3.00 per hour for Mikayla's benefits. What is the cost to *Tomas* for her benefits each week?

g. What is the total cost per hour for Thomas to have Mikayla as an employee?

Running Case Study

Step VII: Labor Cost and Control Techniques

Thomas has learned about labor cost and control techniques. First, he developed a staffing guide for the food servers and the line cooks at *Tomas*. The staffing guide determines the number of employees needed based on customer demand. Then he developed a forecast of customer counts per hour. The last step in this process is to develop employee schedules for the various jobs based on the staffing guide and the forecast of customer counts.

Your assignment is to duplicate the work that Thomas has done for *Tomas* for the restaurant that you are developing. The steps you need to take are as follows:

1. Determine the number of customers your food servers can serve per hour.

2. Determine the number of meals your line cooks can prepare per hour.

3. Determine the number of days per week and hours per day your restaurant will be open.

4. Prepare a forecast of customer counts for your restaurant.

5. Prepare employee schedules for your food servers and line cooks based on the staffing guide and the forecast of customer counts.

Next, prepare the estimated weekly payroll for your employees. Use the following information to prepare the payroll.

1. The average wage rate for food servers and line cooks in your area.

2. The federal, state, and local combined tax rate of 17%.

3. The Social Security rate of 7.5%. Remember, both you and the employee pay this tax.

4. The average cost of benefits for full time employees at $3.25 per hour, per employee.

5. The TRDA for your restaurant is $6.00 per hour.

CHAPTER **14**

Purchasing *and* Inventory Management

> *"Inventory in storage areas is the equivalent of money in the bank."*
>
> —TERRI JONES

Purchasing food, beverages, and other products for the right price and in the right quantities will have a direct impact on a restaurant's profitability. Remember, the price you pay for a food or beverage item determines the food cost and the beverage cost for the menu items. The quantity you purchase can impact the food and beverage costs as well.

LEARNING OBJECTIVES

1. To understand the impact purchasing has on food cost for menu items
2. To understand the impact purchasing has on inventory
3. To understand the impact inventory has on product quality
4. To understand the impact inventory has on cash flow
5. To understand and calculate the cost of goods sold
6. To understand and calculate inventory turnover rates

Purchasing Food Products

The goal of a successful purchasing program is to accurately predict product usage. Food products should be purchased on a regular basis and used within 1 to 10 days after delivery. If this is possible, the quality of the product should not be impacted.

Each time an order is placed with a food supplier, the cost of the items ordered and the cost of delivery must be paid. The delivery charge is then included in the cost of the food for accounting purposes. If orders are placed too often, the cost of delivery can negatively impact (increase) the food cost. Each time a delivery is received and paid for, the cost of the order decreases the amount of cash in the restaurant's bank account. To ensure you have the cash available to pay for the food order, you must manage the purchasing of food items.

Inventory Management

When food, beverages, or other products are delivered to the restaurant, they are placed in the proper storage areas. Frozen foods are placed in the freezer. Fresh meats, seafood, fin fish, dairy, and produce items are placed in refrigerated storage. Canned items, boxed and bagged items, spices, paper products, and so forth are placed in dry storage as shown in Figure 14.1. Cleaning chemicals

FIGURE 14.1

Inventory for Dry Storage
Photography by Thomas Myers

are also placed in dry storage separate from where the food items are stored. Every item placed in a storage area becomes inventory.

Inventory is the term used to describe items purchased for resale or used in the course of doing business. For example, the food products purchased will be used to prepare the menu items served at the restaurant. The paper and cleaning products purchased are either used by the guest as they are served (paper napkins) or used to clean the dishes and so on after the preparation and service of the food. Inventory quantity must be managed to avoid having too much product and therefore too much money tied up within the storage areas.

Tracking of Inventory Quantities

Inventory quantities are tracked using two separate methods. Each method is used to check the accuracy of the other. The first method for tracking inventory is called a perpetual inventory. A **perpetual inventory** is a method that updates inventory quantities every time an item is added to or subtracted from the inventory.

For example, four 50-pound bags of flour are in the dry storage area on June 1, 20XX. An order for six 50-pound bags of flour is received on June 10, 20XX. The perpetual inventory for 50-pound bags of flour is increased by six bags. On June 10, 20XX, there are ten 50-pound bags of flour in inventory.

On June 12, 20XX, the bake shop requisitions two 50-pound bags of flour from their inventory. The quantity of 50-pound bags of flour in inventory is reduced by two bags after the bake shop receives the order. Eight 50-pound bags of flour is the quantity in inventory according to the perpetual inventory information. How is the accuracy of this number verified?

Perpetual Inventory for 50-pound Bags of Flour

Date	Quantity	Value: $20.00/bag
June 1, 20XX	4 bags available	$80.00
June 10, 20XX	6 delivered, 10 bags available	$200.00
June 12, 20XX	2 bags to bake shop, 8 bags available	$160.00

The accuracy of the perpetual inventory is verified by a *physical* inventory. A **physical inventory** is conducted by going into the storage areas and counting every item in inventory. Once each item is counted, the quantities counted are compared to the perpetual inventory balances to ensure the accuracy of the perpetual inventory numbers.

If the quantity of items counted in the physical inventory equals the quantity of items listed on the perpetual inventory forms, the perpetual inventory is correct. However, this is not always the result of the physical inventory. Sometimes the physical inventory quantities do not equal the perpetual inventory quantities. If this is the case, the difference in the quantities, or the **variance**, is investigated.

Let's return to the 50-pound bags of flour. The perpetual inventory form says there are eight 50-pound bags of flour in inventory on June 12, 20XX. The physical inventory taken on June 14, 20XX counts nine 50-pound bags of flour in inventory. Why is there a difference between the perpetual and physical inventory quantities?

In this example, the difference between the perpetual and physical inventory quantities is most likely caused by an employee who only took one 50-pound bag of flour to the bake shop on June 12, 20XX, instead of two. When the variance is discovered, it is corrected by delivering the second bag of flour to the bake shop.

The Importance of Accuracy in Inventory Quantities

Accurate inventory quantities are necessary for effective purchasing management. If the quantity of food items in inventory is incorrect, the quantity of items ordered will also be incorrect. This can result in customers not being able to order their favorite entrée because the restaurant has run out of the ingredients needed to prepare the entrée.

Accurate inventory quantities are necessary for inventory management. If inventory levels are too high, because of inaccurate inventory balances, the dollar value of the inventory may be too high. If the dollar value of inventory is too high, the restaurant may not have enough money in its bank account to pay the other costs of running the business. Remember, the items in inventory have been paid for and they must be prepared and sold in order for the restaurant to earn a profit. If too much product is in inventory, too much cash is tied up in the inventory.

Accurate inventory quantities are necessary for food cost calculations. Inventory quantities and their corresponding costs are used to determine the cost of food sold that appears on the profit and loss statement for a restaurant. Inventory quantities are used to determine both the food cost percent for a menu item and for the overall food cost percent for the restaurant. Food cost calculations depend on accurate inventory information.

Cost of Food Sold Calculations

It is common for a restaurant to prepare a monthly profit and loss statement. The cost of food sold, or the cost of food used for the month, is calculated using purchasing and inventory quantities. The formula is as follows:

> Beginning inventory(BI)
> + Purchases(P)
> Total goods available for sale(GAFS)
> − Ending inventory(EI)
> Cost of food sold(COFS)

The **beginning inventory** is the dollar value of food products in inventory on the first day of the month. The beginning inventory is equal to the ending inventory from the prior month. The dollar value of all food purchased in the month is added to the beginning inventory value. This sum represents the total dollar value of food available for sale during that month.

The last day of every month, a physical inventory is counted. The dollar value of the **ending inventory** is subtracted from the dollar value of the food available for sale. This particular total is the cost of food sold for the month. Following is an example of the cost of food sold calculation.

COST OF FOOD SOLD JUNE 20XX		
June 1, 20XX	Beginning inventory	$3,700.00
	+	
June 1 to 30, 20XX	Purchases	$14,400.00
	Total food available for sale	$18,100.00
	−	
June 30, 20XX	Ending inventory	$4,500.00
	Cost of food sold	$13,600.00

In this example, the cost of food sold for the month of June 20XX is $13,600.00. The dollar amount of $13,600.00 represents the cost for food on the profit and loss statement. The restaurant owner in this example would like to determine his overall food cost percent for June 20XX. The food sales revenue for June 20XX is $54,400.00. The formula for food cost percent is as follows:

Cost of food ÷ Food sales revenue = Food cost percent

$13,600.00 (cost of food) ÷ $54,400.00 (food sales) = .25 or 25% (food cost percent)

The food cost percent is 25%.

This example illustrates how the cost of food sold formula is used to determine the overall food cost percent for a restaurant for one month.

 ## Inventory Turnover Rate

Another calculation used to manage inventory is the **inventory turnover rate**. The inventory turnover rate tells us how often the products in inventory are used. Fresh and frozen food products will deteriorate if they are not used quickly. Therefore, the inventory turnover rate for fresh and frozen food products should be between 3 and 4. An inventory turnover rate of 3 or 4 means that food items are used every 7 to 10 days. This rate ensures that food is being used in a timely manner and that the amount of money tied to inventory is kept to a minimum.

The inventory turnover rate calculation is a two-step process:

STEP 1: Calculate an average based on the beginning and ending inventory for the month:

$$\frac{\text{Beginning inventory} + \text{Ending inventory}}{2} = \text{Average inventory (AI)}$$

STEP 2: Divide the cost of food sold during the month by the average inventory value. The quotient is the inventory turnover rate.

$$\frac{\text{Cost of food used in the month}}{\text{Average inventory for the month}} = \text{Inventory turnover rate}$$

Using the dollar values from the prior example to determine the cost of food sold, we will now do an inventory turnover rate calculation. In the prior example for the cost of food sold, the beginning inventory is $3,700. The ending inventory is $4,500.00. The cost of food sold is $13.600.00.

STEP 1: Calculate an average based on the beginning and ending inventory for the month.

$3,700.00 (BI) + $4,500.00 (EI) = $8,200.00

$$\frac{\$8,200.00}{2} = \$4,100.00 \text{ (average inventory, AI)}$$

The average inventory is $4,100.00

STEP 2: Divide the cost of food sold during the month by the average inventory value.

$$\frac{\$13,600.00 \text{ (COFS)}}{\$4,100.00 \text{ (AI)}} = 3.32 \text{ inventory turnover rate}$$

In this example, the inventory turnover rate is 3.32. The inventory in this restaurant is turning over every 9 days. The formula used to determine the number of days the inventory is turning over is as follows:

$$\frac{30 \text{ (days per month)}}{\text{Inventory turnover rate}} = \text{Number of days food is being used}$$

$$\frac{30 \text{ (days per month)}}{3.32 \text{ (inventory turnover rate)}} = 9 \text{ (days food is being used)}$$

An inventory turnover rate of 3.32, or every 9 days, indicates that the food products are being purchased and used in a timely manner. This turnover rate ensures that the quality of the food is not deteriorating due to extended time in the storage areas. It also ensures the restaurant is doing a good job of managing its cash flow because the food in inventory is being turned into sales revenue every nine days.

 Conclusion

Purchasing and inventory management will have a direct impact on the profitability of a restaurant. A well-managed purchasing program will ensure that food products are received and prepared for sale to guests in a timely manner. A well-managed inventory program will ensure that the products in inventory are turned over every 7 to 10 days. This helps to maintain product quality and assist the restaurant in managing its cash flow.

 **Purchasing and Inventory Management: REVIEW PROBLEMS**

1. Why is it important to manage the purchasing function?

2. Why is it important to manage the quantity of products in inventory?

3. What is the formula used to determine the cost of food sold?

4. Why is the cost of food sold calculation so important for the restaurant operator?

5. What is the difference between a perpetual inventory and a physical inventory?

6. Integrated cost of food sold and inventory turnover rate problem:

	October 20XX	November 20XX
Beginning inventory:	$5,400.00	?
Purchases:	$15,250.00	$18,500.00
Ending inventory:	$4,800.00	$5,200.00

a. What is the dollar value of food available for sale in October?

b. What is the cost of food sold in October?

c. October's sales revenue is $50,000.00. What is the food cost percent for October?

d. What is the beginning inventory for November 20XX?

e. What is the dollar value of food available for sale in November?

f. What is the cost of food sold in November?

g. November's sales revenue is $60,000.00. What is the food cost percent for November?

h. What is the inventory turnover rate for October?

i. How many days did it take to turn over the inventory in October?

j. What is the inventory turnover rate for November?

k. How many days did it take to turn over the inventory in November?

Running Case Study

Step VIII—Purchasing and Inventory Management

T homas is looking at the projected profit and loss statement for *Tomas* for the month of June 20XX. He would like to determine how much food products to purchase each week based on what he has learned by reading Chapter 14.

Tomas Italian Restaurant

Projected Profit and Loss Statement

June 20XX

Sales revenue	
Food	$40,000.00
Beverage	$10,000.00
Total revenue	$50,000.00
Cost of goods sold	
Food	$ 8,000.00
Beverage	$ 1,500.00
Total cost of goods sold	$ 9,500.00

The projected profit and loss statement predicts that *Tomas* will spend $8,000.00 a month on food products. There are 4 weeks in one month. If Thomas divides the $8,000.00 by 4 weeks, he can determine the dollar value for his weekly purchases.

$8,000.00 (cost of food for the month) ÷ 4 (weeks in one month) equals $2,000.00

Thomas should spend $2,000.00 each week purchasing food.

If Thomas does indeed spend $2,000.00 a week purchasing food, he will be properly managing the purchasing function. He will also be managing his inventory because the food in storage will turn over weekly and be replaced by purchasing newer products for his inventory each week.

How much money should you spend each week purchasing food products based on the profit and loss statement for your restaurant?

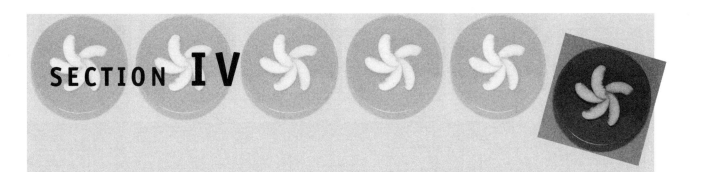

SECTION IV

COMPUTER APPLICATIONS *for the* FOODSERVICE INDUSTRY

CHAPTER 15

Computer Applications
in the **Foodservice Industry**

"The information the computer generates is only valuable if we understand what it means . . ."

—TERRI JONES

Computers are an integral part of the foodservice industry today. The most common computer application in foodservice is the **point-of-sale** (POS) system. Point-of-sale systems are computerized terminals that control the "point of sale" transaction. Another common computer application is **inventory and purchasing software**. This software assists with the mathematics used in the kitchen and with business operations. The size of the foodservice operation and the number of locations where food is sold will determine the type of hardware and software used by the operation. This chapter reviews the computer systems used in foodservice today.

LEARNING OBJECTIVES

1. To identify the advantage of using point-of-sale software in foodservice
2. To list the information the point-of-sale technology provides
3. To identify the advantage of using inventory and purchasing software
4. To list the information the inventory and purchasing software provides
5. To identify computer software used in smaller foodservice operations

The computer technology used in the foodservice industry mirrors the mathematics that has always been a part of the industry. The computer hardware and software programs make the calculations automatic and eliminate the errors caused by simple mistakes. They provide us with a foolproof method for all of the mathematics covered in this book.

The key is still understanding *why* the mathematics is used. This understanding is needed to fully comprehend the information the computer programs are generating. In the precomputer era, the guest check was written on prenumbered paper guest checks and carried into the kitchen. The guest check was added by the food server, sometimes using an adding machine with a tape. At the end of the day, the owner or the manager reviewed the sequence of the prenumbered guest checks and the addition of the items ordered for accuracy. If a guest check was missing from the sequence, an investigation was launched. Did the guest leave without paying, or did the server just make an error on the guest check? The answer determined the server's fate. If there was an error in addition, the food server had to make up the difference. Some small independent operations still utilize this method today.

In the precomputer era, bin cards were common in the storage areas. A **bin card** is a small index card placed in front of every item in storage. The bin cards recorded the perpetual inventory quantities. Each time an item was purchased and added to the inventory, the new items were added to the quantity on the bin card. Each time items were removed from inventory, the quantity was subtracted from the quantity on the bin card. The owner or the manager would conduct a monthly physical inventory to verify the quantity on the bin card and to determine the ending inventory value for the financial statements. This can be a very tedious and time-consuming method for inventory control. Some small independent operators still utilize this method today, but the majority of foodservice operations have entered the age of computers.

Point-of-Sale Technology: The POS System

Point-of-sale computer technology is used at the point where the guest makes a purchase. In a dining room the guest tells the food server which items he or she would like. The food server transfers the guest's request to the point of sale terminal. Then the order is printed in the kitchen. The sale is recorded within the point-of-sale system, along with the amount of money the guest owes for the meal.

When the food is prepared, the server picks up the food and serves the guest. When the guest has finished the meal and is ready to pay, the point-of-sale terminal totals the guest's check. The cashier collects the money, and the ticket is closed.

Point-of-sale technology offers many advantages to the foodservice industry. The POS system adds the guest check without mistakes and can be programmed to collect valuable information useful to running a restaurant. POS technology can also be used as a time clock. Employees can clock in and out of work using the POS terminal. POS technology also tracks total sales revenue, total sales of each food item, and total sales per item, per hour. The sale-per-hour information can prove very helpful with forecasting of customer counts per meal period. This information can also be used to schedule employees for each shift.

Whether POS technology is used in a single-unit restaurant or a single unit of a chain restaurant, it can also track inventory usage, and as a result, it can help to predict the purchasing quantities for the next order. By tracking inventory, the POS system contains the perpetual inventory quantities, which are then verified by a physical inventory. In chain foodservice units, the POS systems have the capability to electronically transfer the sales revenue, payroll, and inventory information to the corporate headquarters, where operational decisions are made.

Multiunit foodservice operations, such as the food and beverage department in a large hotel, or the food outlets at a theme park, use point-of-sale technology at the location where the guests purchase their meals. However, for inventory and purchasing control, a different type of software is used. A foodservice department that is a part of a larger organization generally needs a software package that is more sophisticated than a POS system to handle its inventory and purchasing functions.

Inventory and Purchasing Software Packages: IP Software

In large organizations, the amount of food purchased and included in inventory on a monthly basis can exceed $1 million. Specialized software is used to control this volume of inventory and purchases. This software, called inventory and purchasing (IP) software, tracks inventory quantities (perpetual inventory), purchases, food cost, and which outlet is utilizing particular products, by quantity and cost.

Each unit of the large food and beverage department requisitions product from the overall inventory using the IP software. The IP software tracks the inventory quantity of every product. When the quantity in inventory reaches a predetermined number of units, the item is automatically placed on a list of items that need to be purchased. The simple act of punching a code into the software releases this list of items to purchase. This list can be transferred electronically to the company from which the items are purchased.

In large organizations, a physical inventory is completed daily on a certain portion of the inventory in storage. The reason is that it would be impossible to count the entire inventory at one time. The physical inventory is checked against the perpetual inventory quantities in the IP system to ensure the integrity of the perpetual inventory numbers. As discussed in Chapter 14, any variances between the physical inventory quantities and the perpetual inventory quantities are investigated.

The IP software tracks inventory transfers. For example, in a hotel, food is requisitioned to be prepared by the main kitchen. The prepared food is then transferred to room service, to the coffee shop, and to the employee cafeteria. The portion of the food and the cost of the food transferred to these three locations are entered into the IP system. When the monthly financial statements are prepared, accurate food cost information per food outlet is readily available.

The IP system is also capable of costing a recipe. Once the recipe is entered into the software, the recipe cost is updated each time ingredients are purchased based on the latest cost for the recipe's ingredients. From the recipe cost, the IP system can determine an EP cost of a menu item. If the food cost of these ingredients change dramatically, management will know immediately. Then management can decide to change the menu price or eliminate the item from the menu.

It is important to note that the IP system is capable of performing all of the mathematics necessary to run a successful food and beverage operation. The mathematics used in the kitchen and the mathematics used in the business side of the foodservice industry is incorporated in the IP software. The IP software is a valuable addition to any large foodservice organization.

 ## Menu Printing

Menus are the culmination of the concept of the restaurant as it is presented to the guest. The act of designing and printing menus can be completed using software specifically designed for this purpose. Menus can also be designed utilizing the software already on most computers. A large selection of graphic designs and font styles and sizes are available. This makes menu printing easy and affordable.

 ## Conclusion

Computers are an integral part of the foodservice industry today. Point-of-sale technology provides the foodservice operator with a lot of options to increase the efficiency of the business operation. For larger foodservice operations, IP software incorporates all of the necessary mathematics to run a profitable foodservice operation.

 ## Computer Applications in Foodservice: REVIEW PROBLEMS

1. List the advantages for the foodservice operator of using a point-of-sale system.

2. List the advantages for the foodservice operator of using inventory and purchasing software.

3. Compare and contrast the information received from a point-of-sale system with the information received from precomputer paper guest checks.

4. What type of control procedures should be used with paper guest checks to ensure that all food prepared in the kitchen is paid for by the guest?

Running Case Study

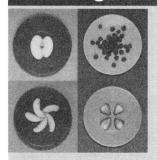

Step IX: Computers at *Tomas*

Thomas has read this chapter, but feels he cannot afford POS or IP software systems at this time. He wonders if he can utilize a desktop or laptop computer for his needs at *Tomas*. The answer is yes.

Thomas can develop spreadsheets using software commonly available on every computer to address all of the operating needs of *Tomas*. He can set up a perpetual inventory system to manage the inventory and purchasing functions. He can record items used and items purchased on a daily basis. On a weekly basis, Thomas can perform a physical inventory to ensure his perpetual and physical inventory quantities are correct.

Thomas can design a spreadsheet that will cost the recipes used at *Tomas*, as well as produce the EP cost. This will help Thomas control his food costs and alert him to price increases in ingredients. Once the spreadsheet is set up, Thomas can use it to develop new menu items based on a certain food cost. This spreadsheet will prove itself very valuable as the business grows.

Thomas can also use his computer to design and print menus. As stated earlier, this is very easy to accomplish.

Thomas's biggest concern will be to make sure that he collects money from every item sold to his guests. This is where he will need to concentrate his efforts. The use of a POS system makes it almost impossible for food to be given to the guest without him or her paying for it. Thomas will need to figure out the best way to ensure that his employees are not forgetting to charge for items sold and to eliminate errors in the addition of the guest checks. If Thomas can devise a system for food ordering and cash collection that is successful, his business has the chance to stand the test of time.

What type of computer and software packages will you use in your restaurant?

Math Facts Multiplication Grid

×	1	2	3	4	5	6	7	8	9	10	11	12
1	1	2	3	4	5	6	7	8	9	10	11	12
2	2	4	6	8	10	12	14	16	18	20	22	24
3	3	6	9	12	15	18	21	24	27	30	33	36
4	4	8	12	16	20	24	28	32	36	40	44	48
5	5	10	15	20	25	30	35	40	45	50	55	60
6	6	12	18	24	30	36	42	48	54	60	66	72
7	7	14	21	28	35	42	49	56	63	70	77	84
8	8	16	24	32	40	48	56	64	72	80	88	96
9	9	18	27	36	45	54	63	72	81	90	99	108
10	10	20	30	40	50	60	70	80	90	100	110	120
11	11	22	33	44	55	66	77	88	99	110	121	132
12	12	24	36	48	60	72	84	96	108	120	132	144
13	13	26	39	52	65	78	91	104	117	130	143	156
14	14	28	42	56	70	84	98	112	126	140	154	168
15	15	30	45	60	75	90	105	120	135	150	165	180

This grid can help you with basic multiplication and division and with common denominators for fractions.

Weight *and* Volume Approximate Measures *of* Food

Foods	1 Ounce Equals	1 Cup Equals	1 Pound Equals
Allspice	$4\frac{1}{2}$ T		
Almonds, shelled		$5\frac{1}{3}$ oz.	3 C
Apples, medium			3 each
Apples, diced			3 C
Applesauce			$1\frac{1}{2}$ C
Apricots, dried		$5\frac{1}{3}$ oz.	3 C
Asparagus, fresh			16 to 18 stalks
Bacon, raw		11 slices	20 to 25 slices
Bacon, fat		8 oz.	2 C
Baking powder	$2\frac{2}{3}$ T	6 oz.	$2\frac{2}{3}$ C
Bananas, medium			3 each
Bananas, diced		$6\frac{1}{2}$ oz.	$2\frac{1}{2}$ C
Beans, green, fresh			1 qt.
Beans, kidney		6 oz.	$2\frac{2}{3}$ C
Beans, lima		$6\frac{1}{2}$ oz.	$2\frac{1}{2}$ C
Beans, navy		7 oz.	$2\frac{1}{4}$ C

Foods	1 Ounce Equals	1 Cup Equals	1 Pound Equals
Beef, cooked, diced		$5\frac{1}{3}$ oz.	3 C
Beef, ground		8 oz.	2 C
Beets, fresh			2–3 each
Beets, cooked		12 oz.	$1\frac{1}{4}$ C
Bran		2 oz.	2 qts.
Bread crumbs, dry		3 oz.	$5\frac{1}{3}$ C
Bread crumbs, soft		2 oz.	2 qts.
Brussels sprouts			1 qt.
Butter	2 T	8 oz.	2 C
Cabbage, shredded		3 oz.	$5\frac{1}{3}$ C
Carrots, small			5–6 each
Carrots, grated, raw		4 oz.	1 qt.
Cauliflower, medium			1 head
Celery		4 oz.	1 qt.
Cheese, American grated		4 oz.	1 qt.
Cheese, cottage		7 oz.	$2\frac{1}{4}$ C
Cheese, cream		4 oz.	1 qt.
Cherries, pie		$5\frac{1}{3}$ oz.	3 C
Cherries, pie, pitted		8 oz.	2 C
Cherries, glacéed		$6\frac{1}{2}$ oz.	$2\frac{1}{2}$ C
Chicken, cooked, diced		$5\frac{1}{3}$ oz.	3 C
Chocolate	1 square		16 squares
Cinnamon	4 T	4 oz.	1 qt.
Citron		$6\frac{1}{2}$ oz.	$2\frac{1}{2}$ C
Cloves, ground	$3\frac{1}{2}$ T	$4\frac{1}{4}$ oz.	$3\frac{3}{4}$ C
Cloves, whole		3 oz.	$5\frac{1}{3}$ C
Cocoa	4 T	4 oz.	1 qt.
Coconut, shredded		2 oz.	2 qts.
Coffee, ground, medium		$3\frac{1}{4}$ oz.	5 C
Cornflakes		1 oz.	1 gal.

Foods	1 Ounce Equals	1 Cup Equals	1 Pound Equals
Cornmeal		5 oz.	$3\frac{1}{4}$ C
Cornstarch	$3\frac{1}{2}$ T	5 oz.	$3\frac{1}{4}$ C
Crab meat		3 oz.	$5\frac{1}{3}$ C
Cracker crumbs		$2\frac{1}{2}$ oz.	$6\frac{1}{3}$ C
Crackers, graham, whole/crushed	18 each	96 each	
Crackers, white soda, 2 × 2	20 each	176 each	
Cranberries		4 oz.	1 qt.
Cream of Wheat		$5\frac{1}{3}$ oz.	3 qts.
Cucumbers			3 medium/3 C
Currants, dried		$5\frac{1}{4}$ oz.	3 C
Dates, pitted		$6\frac{3}{4}$ oz.	2 C
Eggs, hard boiled		4 each	
Eggs, whites		8 oz./7–9 each	14–16 each
Eggs, whole		8 oz./4–5 each	8–10 each
Eggs, yolks		8 oz./12–14 each	24–26 each
Farina, uncooked		$5\frac{1}{3}$ oz.	3 C
Figs, dry		$5\frac{1}{3}$ oz.	3 C
Flour, cake, sifted		$3\frac{1}{2}$ oz.	$4\frac{1}{2}$ C
Flour, graham		$4\frac{1}{2}$ oz.	$3\frac{1}{2}$ C
Flour, rye		$3\frac{1}{2}$ oz.	5 C
Flour, white, sifted		4 oz.	1 qt.
Flour, whole wheat		$5\frac{1}{3}$ oz.	3 C
Gelatin, flavored		$4\frac{1}{2}$ oz.	$3\frac{1}{2}$ C
Gelatin, unflavored	4 T	4 oz.	1 qt.
Ginger, crystallized, cut fine	1 T		
Ginger, dry	5 T		
Grapes, seeded, cut			$2\frac{3}{4}$ C
Grapefruit			2 C
Ham, ground		8 oz.	2 C
Hominy, pearl		$5\frac{1}{3}$ oz.	3 C

Foods	1 Ounce Equals	1 Cup Equals	1 Pound Equals
Horseradish, prepared		4 oz.	1 qt.
Lemons, medium			3–4
Lemon juice		8 oz.	2 C/8 lemons
Lemon peel	4 T		
Lettuce, average head		8–9 oz.	
Macaroni, dry		$3\frac{1}{2}$ oz.	$4\frac{1}{2}$ C
Marshmallows			60 each
Mayonnaise		$7\frac{1}{4}$ oz.	
Milk		8 oz.	2 C
Molasses			$1\frac{1}{3}$ C
Mushrooms, fresh			$1\frac{1}{3}$ qts.
Mushrooms, sautéed			$1\frac{1}{2}$ C
Mustard, dry	5 T	$3\frac{1}{4}$ oz.	5 C
Noodles, dry			3 qts.
Nutmeg, ground	$3\frac{1}{2}$ T	$4\frac{1}{2}$ oz.	$3\frac{1}{2}$ C
Oats, rolled		3 oz.	$5\frac{1}{3}$ C
Oil, corn		7 oz.	$2\frac{1}{4}$ C
Olives, green, diced		20 each	
Olives, ride, diced		44 each	
Olives, stuffed		56 each	
Onions, chopped		8 oz.	2 C/4–5 medium
Orange juice		4 each	
Orange peel	3 T		
Oysters			1 qt. large, 40–45
Paprika	4 T	4 oz.	1 qt.
Peaches, fresh, medium			3–4 each
Peanut butter		9 oz.	$1\frac{3}{4}$ C
Pears, medium			3–4 each
Pecans		$3\frac{1}{2}$ oz.	$4\frac{1}{2}$ C
Pepper, white	4 T	4 oz.	1 qt.

Foods	1 Ounce Equals	1 Cup Equals	1 Pound Equals
Peppers, green, chopped		2–3 each	
Pickles, chopped		12 small	
Pimientos		7 oz./4 diced	
Pineapple, sliced, canned		3 slices, drained	8–12 slices
Pineapple juice		8 oz.	2 C
Pork, ground			2 C
Potatoes, white, raw, medium			3–4 each
Potatoes, white, cooked, drained		2 C	
Prunes, cooked			3 C, drained
Prunes, dried			$2\frac{1}{2}$ C
Pumpkin, canned		8 oz.	2 C
Raisins, seedless		$5\frac{1}{3}$ oz.	3 C
Rice, uncooked		8 oz.	2 C
Rice, cooked			2 qts.
Rhubarb, sliced		4 oz.	1 qt.
Salad dressing, French		8 oz.	2 C
Salmon, canned			2 C
Salt	2 T	8 oz.	2 C
Shortening		$6\frac{1}{2}$ oz.	$2\frac{1}{2}$ C
Shrimp		5 oz.	$3\frac{1}{3}$ C
Soda	$2\frac{1}{3}$ T		
Spaghetti, dry		4 oz.	1 qt.
Spinach, cooked			$2\frac{1}{2}$ C
Squash, Hubbard, cooked			$2\frac{1}{2}$ C
Strawberries, crushed			2 C
Strawberries, fresh, whole			3 C
Sugar, brown		6 oz.	$2\frac{3}{4}$ C
Sugar, confectioner's		$5\frac{1}{3}$ oz.	3 C
Sugar, cubes			120 each
Sugar, granulated		8 oz.	2 C

Foods	1 Ounce Equals	1 Cup Equals	1 Pound Equals
Tapioca, instant		$6\frac{3}{4}$ oz.	$2\frac{1}{2}$ C
Tapioca, pearl		$5\frac{1}{3}$ oz.	3 C
Tea		2 oz.	
Tomatoes, canned		8 oz.	2 C
Tomatoes, fresh, medium			3–4 each
Tomato juice		8 oz.	2 C
Tomato puree		$8\frac{1}{2}$ oz.	
Tuna fish		8 oz.	2 C
Vanilla wafers, crushed			5 C
Veal, ground		8 oz.	2 C
Vinegar		8 oz.	2 C
Walnuts		4 oz.	1 qt.
Yeast, compresses		2 cakes	

Average Yield Percent Chart

Item	Average Yield Percent	Item	Average Yield Percent
Fruit		**Vegetables (cont.)**	
Apples	85%	Eggplant	84%
Apricots	92%	Garlic	88%
Bananas	66%	Lettuce:	
Blackberries, fresh	95%	Iceberg	73%
Blackberries, frozen	100%	Leaf	81%
Blueberries, fresh	90%	Romaine	75%
Blueberries, frozen	100%	Mushrooms	94%
Cherries, fresh	88%	Onions:	
Cranberries, fresh	96%	Large	91%
Grapes, green	94%	Small	88%
Grapes, red	89%	Peppers, green	81%
Kiwi	85%	Potatoes	78%
Mango	69%	Sweet potatoes	75%
Melon:		Tomatoes, sliced	94%
Cantaloupe	58%		
Honeydew	58%	**Meats**	
Watermelon	50%	Beef	
Nectarines	75%	Prime rib roast	50%
Peaches	78%	Top round	75%
Pears	76%	Tri tip	63%
Pineapple	48%	Pork	
Raspberries	96%	Pork loin, whole	53%
Strawberries	92%	Pork loin, boneless	75%
Vegetables		**Fin Fish**	
Asparagus	57%	Sea bass, drawn	50%
Avocado	79%	Salmon, dressed	75%
Belgian endive	83%	Tuna, dressed	65%
Broccoli	63%		
Cabbage	80%	**Poultry**	
Carrots	81%	Chicken, whole	
Cauliflower	60%	Breast	30%
Celery	69%	Wings	11%
Cucumbers	95%	Legs	28%

Standardized Recipe
Cost Form

Recipe Yield:

Portion Size:

Number of Portions:

Total Cost:

Cost per Portion:

Date: June 20XX

Item	Item Quantity	AP Unit of Measure	AP Cost per Unit	÷	Average Yield Percent (or Other Unit of Measure Info)	=	EP Cost per Unit	×	Item Quantity	=	Recipe Item Cost
				÷		=		×		=	
				÷		=		×		=	
				÷		=		×		=	
				÷		=		×		=	
				÷		=		×		=	

Recipe cost   =

Recipe cost plus 2% for misc. items =

Recipe Yield:
Portion Size:
Number of Portions:

Total Cost:
Cost per Portion:
Date: June 20XX

Item	Item Quantity	AP Unit of Measure	AP Cost per Unit	÷	Average Yield Percent (or Other Unit of Measure Info)	=	EP Cost per Unit	×	Item Quantity	=	Recipe Item Cost
				÷		=		×		=	
				÷		=		×		=	
				÷		=		×		=	
				÷		=		×		=	
				÷		=		×		=	

Recipe cost =

Recipe cost plus 2% for misc. items =

Projected Profit *and* Loss Sample Statement *and* Form

Tomas Italian Restaurant

Projected Profit and Loss Statement
June 20XX

	Dollars	Percentage
Sales Revenue		
Food	$40,000.00	80%
Beverage	$10,000.00	20%
Total Revenue	$50,000.00	100%
Cost of Sales		
Cost of Food	$ 8,000.00	20% of $40,000 (food cost)
Cost of Beverage	$ 1,500.00	15% of $10,000 (beverage cost)
Total Cost of Sales	$ 9,500.00	

[$50,000.00 (total revenue) − $9,500.00 (total cost) = $40,500.00]

Gross Profit	$40,500.00	
Operating Expenses		
Salaries and Wages	$12,000.00	24% of $50,000 (direct labor cost)
Employee Benefits	$ 3,000.00	6% of $50,000 (benefit cost)
China, Glassware, Flatware, Linens	$ 50.00	
Cleaning Supplies	$ 295.00	
Uniforms	$ 525.00	
Menus	$ 0.00	
Paper Products	$ 400.00	
Administrative and General	$ 255.00	
Marketing and Advertising	$ 50.00	
Operations and Maintenance	$ 325.00	
Utilities	$ 1,200.00	
Total Operating Expenses	$18,100.00	

[$40,500.00 (gross profit) − $18,100.00 (total operating expenses) = $22,400.00]

Income Before Capital Expenses	$22,400.00	
Capital Expenses		
Insurance	$ 750.00	
Rent	$ 4,000.00	
Real Estate Taxes	$ 800.00	
Interest Expense	$ 1,450.00	
Depreciation	$ 2,900.00	
Total Capital Expenses	$ 9,900.00	

[$22,400.00 (income before capital expenses) − $9,900.00 (capital expenses) = $12,500.00]

Profit Before Income Taxes	$12,500.00	

Your Restaurant

Projected Profit and Loss Statement **June 20XX**		
	Dollars	**Percentage**
Sales Revenue		
Food	$	
Beverage	$	
Total Revenue	$	
Cost of Sales		
Cost of Food	$	
Cost of Beverage	$	
Total Cost of Sales	$	
[(total revenue) – (total cost) =]		
Gross Profit	$	
Operating Expenses		
Salaries and Wages	$	
Employee Benefits	$	
China, Glassware, Flatware, Linens	$	
Cleaning Supplies	$	
Uniforms	$	
Menus	$	
Paper Products	$	
Administrative and General	$	
Marketing and Advertising	$	
Operations and Maintenance	$	
Utilities	$	
Total Operating Expenses	$	
[(gross profit) – (total operating expenses) =]		
Income Before Capital Expenses	$	
Capital Expenses		
Insurance	$	
Rent	$	
Real Estate Taxes	$	
Interest Expense	$	
Depreciation	$	
Total Capital Expenses	$	
[(income before capital expenses) – (capital expenses) =]		
Profit Before Income Taxes	$	

Your Restaurant

	Projected Profit and Loss Statement June 20XX	
	Dollars	**Percentage**
Sales Revenue		
Food	$	
Beverage	$	
Total Revenue	$	
Cost of Sales		
Cost of Food	$	
Cost of Beverage	$	
Total Cost of Sales	$	
[(total revenue) – (total cost) =]		
Gross Profit	$	
Operating Expenses		
Salaries and Wages	$	
Employee Benefits	$	
China, Glassware, Flatware, Linens	$	
Cleaning Supplies	$	
Uniforms	$	
Menus	$	
Paper Products	$	
Administrative and General	$	
Marketing and Advertising	$	
Operations and Maintenance	$	
Utilities	$	
Total Operating Expenses	$	
[(gross profit) – (total operating expenses) =]		
Income Before Capital Expenses	$	
Capital Expenses		
Insurance	$	
Rent	$	
Real Estate Taxes	$	
Interest Expense	$	
Depreciation	$	
Total Capital Expenses	$	
[(income before capital expenses) – (capital expenses) =]		
Profit Before Income Taxes	$	

Equivalent Units, Conversion Tables, *and* Sizes *and* Capacities Charts

Decimal Equivalent for Fractions of a Unit

Whole units are on the left.	The fraction of part of the unit is on the right.
If the whole units are:	The decimal equivalents are part of:
Ounces	1 pound
Tablespoons	1 cup
Cups	1 gallon

Fraction Part of the Unit

Number of Units	+ ¼ of Unit	+ ⅓ of Unit	+ ½ of Unit	+ ⅔ of Unit	+ ¾ of Unit
0	—	0.02	0.02	0.03	0.04	0.05
1	0.06	.08	.08	.09	.10	.11
2	.12	.14	.15	.16	.17	.17
3	.19	.20	.21	.22	.23	.23
4	.25	.27	.27	.28	.29	.30
5	.31	.33	.33	.34	.35	.36
6	.38	.39	.40	.41	.42	.42
7	.44	.45	.46	.47	.48	.48

Fraction Part of the Unit (Continued)

Number of Units	+ ¼ of Unit	+ ⅓ of Unit	+ ½ of Unit	+ ⅔ of Unit	+ ¾ of Unit
8	.50	.52	.52	.53	.54	.55
9	.56	.58	.58	.59	.60	.61
10	.62	.64	.65	.66	.67	.67
11	.69	.70	.71	.72	.73	.73
12	.75	.77	.77	.78	.79	.80
13	.81	.83	.83	.84	.85	.86
14	.88	.89	.90	.91	.92	.92
15	.94	.95	.96	.97	.98	.98
16	1.00	1.02	1.02	1.03	1.04	1.05

Decimal Weight Equivalents

Ounces		Pounds		Ounces		Pounds
1 oz.	=	0.06 lb.		16 oz.	=	1.00 lb.
2 oz.	=	0.12 lb.		32 oz.	=	2.00 lb.
3 oz.	=	0.19 lb.		35 oz.	=	2.19 lb.
4 oz.	=	0.25 lb.		48 oz.	=	3.00 lb.
5 oz.	=	0.31 lb.		64 oz.	=	4.00 lb.
6 oz.	=	0.38 lb.		71 oz.	=	4.44 lb.
7 oz.	=	0.44 lb.		80 oz.	=	5.00 lb.
8 oz.	=	0.50 lb.		96 oz.	=	6.00 lb.
9 oz.	=	0.56 lb.		106 oz.	=	6.63 lb.
10 oz.	=	0.62 lb.		112 oz.	=	7.00 lb.
11 oz.	=	0.69 lb.		128 oz.	=	8.00 lb.
12 oz.	=	0.75 lb.		141 oz.	=	8.82 lb.
13 oz.	=	0.81 lb.		144 oz.	=	9.00 lb.
14 oz.	=	0.88 lb.		160 oz.	=	10.00 lb.
15 oz.	=	0.94 lb.				

U.S. Volume Equivalents for Liquids

1 tablespoon (T, tbsp.)	= 3 teaspoons (t, tsp.)	= 0.5 fluid ounces (fl. oz.)
1/8 cup (C, c)	= 2 tablespoons	= 1 fluid ounce
1/4 cup	= 4 tablespoons	= 2 fluid ounces
1/3 cup	= 5 1/3 tablespoons	= 2.65 fluid ounces
3/8 cup	= 6 tablespoons	= 3 fluid ounces
1/2 cup	= 8 tablespoons	= 4 fluid ounces
5/8 cup	= 10 tablespoons	= 5 fluid ounces
2/3 cup	= 10 2/3 tablespoons	= 5.3 fluid ounces
3/4 cup	= 12 tablespoons	= 6 fluid ounces
7/8 cup	= 14 tablespoons	= 7 fluid ounces
1 cup	= 16 tablespoons	= 8 fluid ounces
1/2 pint (pt)	= 1 cups	= 8 fluid ounces
1 pint	= 2 cups	= 16 fluid ounces
1 quart (qt.)	= 2 pints	= 32 fluid ounces
1 gallon (G, gal.)	= 4 quarts	= 128 fluid ounces
1 peck	= 8 quarts, dry	
1 bushel	= 4 pecks	

Metric to U.S. Equivalents by Volume

Liter (L)	Milliliter (mL)	Fluid Ounces (fl. oz.)	Gallon (G, gal.)	Quart (Qt.)	Pint (Pt.)	Cup (C, c)	Tablespoon (T, tbsp.)	Teaspoon (t, tsp.)
3.8 L	3,800 mL	128 fl. oz.	1 gal.	4 qts.	8 pt.	16 C		
1 L	1,000 mL	33.8 fl. oz.						
0.95 L	946 mL	32 fl. oz.	.25 gal.	1 qt.	2 pt.	4 C		
	750 mL	25.4 fl. oz.						
	500 mL	16.9 fl. oz.						
.47 L	474 mL	16 fl. oz.		.5 qt.	1 pt.	2 C		
.24 L	237 mL	8 fl. oz.			.5 pt.	1 C		
	30 mL	1 fl. oz.						
	15 mL						1 T	
	5 mL							1 tsp.

Metric Equivalent by Weight

U.S. Unit	Metric Unit
Ounces (oz.)	*Grams (g)*
1 ounce	28.35 g
4 ounces	113.4 g
8 ounces	226.8 g
16 ounces	453.6 g
Pounds (lb, #)	*Grams (g)*
1 pound	453.6 g
2 pounds	907.2 g
2.2 pounds	1,000 g (1 kilogram)

U.S./Metric Conversion Multipliers

Multiply	By	To Find
Volume Units		
Gallons	3.7853	Liters
Liters	1.0567	Quarts
Quarts	.946	Liters
Pints	.474	Liters
Cups	.237	Liters
Weight Units		
Kilograms	2.2046	Pounds
Pounds	.4536	Kilograms
Grams	.0022	Pounds
Pounds	453.5924	Grams
Grams	.0353	Ounces
Ounces	28.3495	Grams

Size and Capacities of Ladles

Number on Ladle	Approximate Measure
1 ounce	⅛ (.125) C
2 ounces	¼ (.25) C
4 ounces	½ (.5) C
6 ounces	¾ (.75) C
8 ounces	1 C
12 ounces	1½ (1.5) C

Size and Capacities of Scoops (Dishers)

Number on Scoop (Disher)	Level Measure
6	⅔ (.67) C
8	½ (.5) C
10	⅜ (.375) C
12	⅓ (.33) C
16	¼ (.25) C
20	3⅓ tablespoons
24	2⅔ tablespoons
30	2 tablespoons
40	1⅔ tablespoons
50	3¾ teaspoons
60	3¼ teaspoons
70	2¾ teaspoons
100	2 teaspoons

Size and Capacities of Measuring/Serving Spoons

Size of Measuring/Serving Spoons	Approximate Measure
2 ounces	¼ (.25) C
3 ounces	⅜ (.375) C
4 ounces	½ (.5) C
6 ounces	¾ (.75) C
8 ounces	1 C

GLOSSARY

A

À la carte A menu pricing method where each item is priced individually.

As purchased (AP) The food or beverage item as it is purchased from the supplier. The item, as purchased, has an AP price and an AP weight, volume, or count.

As served (AS) The exact amount of food or beverage served to the guest. There is an AS quantity, in weight, volume, or count, and an AS price.

Average guest check The amount of money the guest spends, on average, on a meal in a restaurant. The average guest check will vary by meal period.

B

Beverage cost The price paid for alcoholic and nonalcoholic beverage products. The beverage cost can be determined per menu item, per day, per week, per month, or per year. The total cost of beverage per accounting period appears on the profit and loss statement.

Beverage cost percent The cost of the beverage product in relation to the menu price. The beverage cost percent applies to nonalcoholic and alcoholic beverages. The beverage cost percent can be determined per item, per day, per week, per month, or per year.

Bin cards The manual system used to track the quantity of items in inventory. Bin cards are located in the storage areas. Each item's quantity is adjusted on the bin card every time items are added to or subtracted from inventory.

Butcher's yield test The process of determining the dollar value of meat or poultry items that are fabricated on-site. This determination is then compared to the current market value for these same cuts of meat or poultry purchased already fabricated. The cost of labor should be considered in this cost comparison.

C

Call liquor A mid-range-quality and mid-priced alcoholic beverage product. Call liquor is generally located behind the bar on the bottom and middle shelves.

Cash flow The actual amount of money collected and spent by a business.

Common factor A number that can be divided evenly into both the numerator and the denominator of a fraction.

Computerized beverage control system A computer system that integrates the quantity of liquor poured with a cash control component.

Contribution margin pricing method A menu pricing method that equally shares the cost of doing business with every menu item.

Conversion factor The number used to multiply all of a recipe's ingredients in order to adjust the yield of the recipe. It is the quotient of the formula: New yield ÷ Old yield.

Cost of food sold The dollar value of the amount of food prepared and served to the guest during an accounting period.

Cost of sale The actual dollar cost of the food and/or beverage served to a guest. The cost of the sale can be determined by the menu item, daily, weekly, or monthly. The total cost of sale per accounting period appears on the profit and loss statement.

Cost per portion The total cost of the food served to the guest.

Count The number of units of a product. The number of units can be AP units per pound or per case, or can be the number of units per recipe or per portion.

D

Decimal A linear array of integers that represent a fraction.

Decimal number A number that uses a decimal point and place value to show a value less than 1.

Denominator The bottom number in a fraction.

Dividend The number to be divided in a division problem.

Divisor The number the dividend is divided by in a division problem.

Directs Food or beverage items that are received and go directly into production. Directs never enter inventory. Their cost is considered in the daily food cost the day they are received. Their cost must be added to the monthly food cost.

E

Edible portion (EP) The amount of AP food product that remains after fabrication and cooking. The edible portion is the actual food that is served to the guest. The edible portion has its own price per unit of measure; weight, volume, or count.

Entrée Main course of a meal.

Estimate A rough or approximate calculation.

F

Fabricated Food products that are recipe ready. These products are cleaned, trimmed, sliced, and so on and are ready to add to a recipe or serve to the guest.

Factor One or more quantities that divide a given quantity without a remainder.

Fluid ounce (fl. oz.) A volume unit of measure common in the United States.

Food cost The cost of food purchased for sale to the guest. The food cost can be determined per menu item, per day, per week, per month, or per year. The total cost of food per accounting period appears on the profit and loss statement.

Food cost percent The cost of the food in relation to its menu price. The food cost percent can be determined per menu item, per day, per week, per month, or per year.

Fraction A quotient of two quantities shown as a numerator over a denominator.

G

Greater than (>) A symbol that expresses that one number is larger than another.

Gross profit Profit after the cost of sale is subtracted from total sales revenue.

I

Improper fraction A fraction whose numerator is equal to or greater than the denominator.

Ingredient One or more parts of a recipe.

Integer A member of the set of positive or negative whole numbers and zero.

Inventory Food, beverage, and supplies that are in storage and available for use in a foodservice operation. As products are removed from inventory, their cost is transferred from inventory to cost of sale.

Inventory purchasing software A computer program that tracks inventory quantities and value. Commonly referred to as an IP system, it is used in large food and beverage operations.

L

Least common denominator The smallest number that can be divided evenly by two or more fractions' denominators. Also called lowest common denominator.

Least common multiple The smallest quantity exactly divisible by two or more given quantities. The smallest number that is a multiple of two or more numbers. Also called lowest common multiple.

Less than (<) A symbol that expresses one number is smaller than another.

Liquor pouring gun A mechanical device that controls and measures the flow of liquor. The handheld device is called a gun.

Lowest common denominator See Least common dominator.

Lowest common multiple See Least common multiple.

M

Margin of error A certain number of units above the estimated amount. The extra units are available if demand is higher than predicted.

Menu A list of items available for sale in a restaurant. Each menu item has its own price per portion served to the guest.

Metric system Units of measure that are based on the number 10. The metric system is used globally, except in the United States, which has yet to fully adopt it.

Mise en place From the French for "setting in place," the gathering and placement of the tools and product needed to produce an item.

Mixed number The sum of a whole number greater than zero and a proper fraction.

Multiple A quantity that can be divided into a number without a remainder.

Multiplier A quantity by which another number is multiplied.

Multiplicand A number in a multiplication equation.

N

Noninteger number A quantity that is not a whole number.

Numerator The top number in a fraction.

O

One-price method A menu pricing method where like items are all the same price.

Operating results The profit or loss a business produces in a set period of time.

P

Percent The amount or rate per 100, represented with a percent sign: %.

Perpetual inventory A system for tracking item quantities and values in inventory.

Physical inventory The act of counting every item in inventory. The physical inventory is compared to the perpetual inventory, and variances are investigated.

Point-of-sale system A computer system used in foodservice to record sales, print orders in the kitchen, track payroll, and track inventory.

Portion The size of one serving of food sold to a guest.

Premium liquor The highest-quality and highest-priced liquor sold at a beverage operation. Premium liquor is usually located on the top shelf behind the bar.

Primal cut One of the primary divisions for cutting meat carcasses into smaller pieces.

Prime number A whole number that has itself and 1 as its only factors.

Prix fixe A menu pricing method that includes the entire meal for one price.

Product The number obtained by multiplying one quantity by another.

Profit and loss statement A standardized accounting document that lists a business's revenue and expenses.

Projection An estimate of future possibilities based on current trends.

Proper fraction A fraction whose numerator is less than the denominator.

Proportion The relationship of one part to another; equality between two ratios.

Purchase To buy food, beverage, or supplies for a restaurant.

Q

Quantity The amount of product; can be AP, EP, or AS.

Quotient The number obtained by dividing one quantity by another.

R

Ratio The comparison of two numbers or the quotient of two numbers. A ratio can be expressed as a fraction, as a division problem, or as an expression, such as 1 to 2.

Recipe ready Ingredients in the state needed to prepare a recipe. For example, diced onions are recipe ready.

Recipe yield The quantity of food or number of portions a properly prepared recipe produces.

Reciprocal   Either of a pair of numbers whose product is 1; $\frac{1}{4}$ and $\frac{4}{1}$ are reciprocals.

Remainder   The quantity that remains in a division equation.

Requisition   A written request for food, beverage, or supplies located in inventory.

Rounding   The adjusting of a decimal number to its tenth or hundredth place.

S

Sales revenue   The money collected in a restaurant from selling food and beverage items.

Safety level   Extra units of product. These extra units are available if the demand for a product is greater than anticipated.

Scale   An instrument used to measure the weight of an item.

Standardized recipe   Recipes used in the foodservice industry that ensure the consistency and cost of a menu item.

T

Table d'hôte   A menu pricing method that includes the entire meal for one price.

Total recipe cost   The cost of all of the ingredients in a recipe.

Trim   The amount of waste cut off of a food product.

V

Variance   A difference between two numbers that should be equal.

W

Weight   The heaviness of an item. Weight is measured on a scale.

Well liquor   The lowest-quality, lowest-priced liquor sold in a beverage operation. This is the product in the well behind the bar.

Whole number   An integer.

Y

Yield percent   The percent of the AP quantity that is edible.

Yield test   The actual process of determining the edible portion of an item from its as purchased state. The item is weighted AP and again when it is ready to be served to the guest.

ANSWERS TO EVEN-NUMBERED PROBLEMS

CHAPTER 1

Addition:

2. 267 + 389 = 656

4. 1,117 + 206 = 1,323

6.
$$\begin{array}{r} 1,245 \\ +\ 2,456 \\ \hline 3,701 \end{array}$$

8.
$$\begin{array}{r} 10,538 \\ +\ 12,662 \\ \hline 23,200 \end{array}$$

10.
$$\begin{array}{r} 1,650,324 \\ +\ 2,895,421 \\ \hline 4,545,745 \end{array}$$

Subtraction:

2. 54 − 33 = 21

4. 1,064 − 889 = 175

6.
$$\begin{array}{r} 654 \\ -\ 550 \\ \hline 104 \end{array}$$

8.
$$\begin{array}{r} 15,693 \\ -\ 9,872 \\ \hline 5,821 \end{array}$$

10.
$$\begin{array}{r} 5,678,321 \\ -\ 2,889,450 \\ \hline 2,788,871 \end{array}$$

Multiplication:

2. 45 × 4 = 180

4. 1,234 × 5 = 6,170

6.
$$\begin{array}{r} 65 \\ \times\ 5 \\ \hline 325 \end{array}$$

8.
$$\begin{array}{r} 250 \\ \times\ 4 \\ \hline 1,000 \end{array}$$

10.
$$\begin{array}{r} 2,500 \\ \times\ 60 \\ \hline 150,000 \end{array}$$

Division:

2. 60 ÷ 12 = 5

4. $\dfrac{90}{45} = 2$

6. 1,200 ÷ 300 = 4

8. $\dfrac{2004}{12} = 167$

10. 25,000 ÷ 25 = 1,000

12. $\dfrac{800}{400} = 2$

CHAPTER 2

2. How many long white tablecloths are needed? 1 per table = 40

4. What is the total number of tablecloths that need to be ordered? 2 per table = 80

6. How many blue napkins are needed? Every other guest has a blue napkin: 400 ÷ 2 = 200

8. What is the total number of knives, forks, and spoons needed to set the tables?

> There are 400 guests.
> Knives: $400 \times 2 = 800$
> Forks: $400 \times 3 = 1{,}200$
> Spoons: $400 \times 4 = 1{,}600$

10. How many racks of water goblets, champagne glasses, and coffee cups are needed to set the tables?

> There are 25 water goblets per rack: $400 \div 25 = 16$
> There are 30 champagne glasses per rack: $400 \div 30 = 13.33$, rounded to 14
> There are 20 coffee cups per rack: $400 \div 20 = 20$

CHAPTER 3

Convert the following improper fractions to mixed numbers.

2. $\dfrac{10}{8} = 1\dfrac{1}{4}$

4. $\dfrac{4}{2} = 2$

6. $\dfrac{100}{50} = 2$

8. $\dfrac{15}{5} = 3$

10. $\dfrac{22}{8} = 2\dfrac{3}{4}$

12. $\dfrac{10}{4} = 2\dfrac{1}{2}$

14. $\dfrac{40}{5} = 8$

Convert the following fractions to a decimal and a percent.

2. $\dfrac{1}{4} = .25$ or 25%

4. $\dfrac{1}{5} = .20$ or 25%

6. $\dfrac{1}{8} = .125$ or 12.5%

8. $\dfrac{3}{5} = .60$ or 60%

10. $\dfrac{2}{3} = .667$ or 66.7% (.666 rounded to .667)

12. $\dfrac{2}{4} = .50$ or 50%

14. $\dfrac{6}{10} = .60$ or 60%

Convert the following decimals to a percent and a fraction.

2. $.20 = 20\%$ or $\dfrac{1}{5}$

4. $.25 = 25\%$ or $\dfrac{1}{4}$

6. $.40 = 40\% \text{ or } \dfrac{4}{10}$

8. $1.00 = 100\% \text{ or } \dfrac{1}{1}$

10. $.65 = 65\% \text{ or } \dfrac{65}{100}$

12. $.87 = 87\% \text{ or } \dfrac{87}{100}$

14. $.75 = 75\% \text{ or } \dfrac{75}{100}$

Convert the following percents to a decimal and a fraction.

2. $88\% = .88 \text{ or } \dfrac{88}{100}$

4. $18\% = .18 \text{ or } \dfrac{18}{100}$

6. $15\% = .15 \text{ or } \dfrac{15}{100}$

8. $30\% = .30 \text{ or } \dfrac{30}{100}$

10. $10\% = .10 \text{ or } \dfrac{10}{100} = \dfrac{1}{10}$

12. $35\% = .35 \text{ or } \dfrac{35}{100}$

14. $23\% = .23 \text{ or } \dfrac{23}{100}$

CHAPTER 4

Addition of fractions with a common denominator

2. $\dfrac{1}{3} + \dfrac{2}{3} = \dfrac{3}{3} = 1$

4. $\dfrac{5}{9} + \dfrac{8}{9} = \dfrac{13}{9} = 1\dfrac{4}{9}$

6. $\dfrac{2}{7} + \dfrac{4}{7} = \dfrac{6}{7}$

8. $\dfrac{4}{9} + \dfrac{3}{9} = \dfrac{7}{9}$

10. $\dfrac{3}{4} + \dfrac{3}{4} = \dfrac{6}{4} = 1\dfrac{2}{4} = 1\dfrac{1}{2}$

12. $\dfrac{9}{14} + \dfrac{9}{14} = \dfrac{18}{14} = 1\dfrac{4}{14} = 1\dfrac{2}{7}$

14. $\dfrac{7}{10} + \dfrac{9}{10} = \dfrac{16}{10} = 1\dfrac{6}{10} = 1\dfrac{3}{5}$

Addition of fractions without a common denominator

2. $\dfrac{3}{5} + \dfrac{8}{15} = \dfrac{9}{15} + \dfrac{8}{15} = \dfrac{17}{15} = 1\dfrac{2}{15}$

4. $\dfrac{1}{4} + \dfrac{1}{3} = \dfrac{3}{12} + \dfrac{4}{12} = \dfrac{7}{12}$

6. $\dfrac{1}{8} + \dfrac{3}{24} = \dfrac{3}{24} + \dfrac{3}{24} = \dfrac{6}{24} = \dfrac{1}{4}$

8. $\dfrac{1}{9} + \dfrac{5}{18} = \dfrac{2}{18} + \dfrac{5}{18} = \dfrac{7}{18}$

10. $\dfrac{2}{7}+\dfrac{7}{21}=\dfrac{6}{21}+\dfrac{7}{21}=\dfrac{13}{21}$

14. $\dfrac{9}{11}+\dfrac{9}{22}=\dfrac{18}{22}+\dfrac{9}{22}=\dfrac{27}{22}=1\dfrac{5}{22}$

12. $\dfrac{1}{2}+\dfrac{1}{8}=\dfrac{4}{8}+\dfrac{1}{8}=\dfrac{5}{8}$

Subtraction of fractions with a common denominator

2. $\dfrac{7}{10}-\dfrac{5}{10}=\dfrac{2}{10}=\dfrac{1}{5}$

10. $\dfrac{13}{14}-\dfrac{9}{14}=\dfrac{4}{14}=\dfrac{2}{7}$

4. $\dfrac{2}{3}-\dfrac{1}{3}=\dfrac{1}{3}$

12. $\dfrac{15}{16}-\dfrac{5}{16}=\dfrac{10}{16}=\dfrac{5}{8}$

6. $\dfrac{5}{9}-\dfrac{2}{9}=\dfrac{3}{9}=\dfrac{1}{3}$

14. $\dfrac{9}{14}-\dfrac{5}{14}=\dfrac{4}{14}=\dfrac{2}{7}$

8. $\dfrac{3}{24}-\dfrac{1}{24}=\dfrac{2}{24}=\dfrac{1}{12}$

Subtraction of fractions without a common denominator

2. $\dfrac{2}{10}-\dfrac{1}{5}=\dfrac{2}{10}-\dfrac{2}{10}=0$

10. $\dfrac{3}{8}-\dfrac{3}{16}=\dfrac{6}{16}-\dfrac{3}{16}=\dfrac{3}{16}$

4. $\dfrac{1}{2}-\dfrac{1}{8}=\dfrac{4}{8}-\dfrac{1}{8}=\dfrac{3}{8}$

12. $\dfrac{9}{20}-\dfrac{1}{5}=\dfrac{9}{20}-\dfrac{4}{20}=\dfrac{5}{20}=\dfrac{1}{4}$

6. $\dfrac{3}{8}-\dfrac{1}{16}=\dfrac{6}{16}-\dfrac{1}{16}=\dfrac{5}{16}$

14. $\dfrac{1}{2}-\dfrac{1}{4}=\dfrac{2}{4}-\dfrac{1}{4}=\dfrac{1}{4}$

8. $\dfrac{11}{12}-\dfrac{19}{24}=\dfrac{22}{24}-\dfrac{19}{24}=\dfrac{3}{24}=\dfrac{1}{8}$

Multiplication of fractions

2. $\dfrac{1}{4}\times\dfrac{1}{8}=\dfrac{1}{32}$

10. $\dfrac{2}{7}\times\dfrac{1}{8}=\dfrac{2}{56}=\dfrac{1}{28}$

4. $\dfrac{1}{2}\times\dfrac{1}{2}=\dfrac{1}{4}$

12. $\dfrac{2}{3}\times\dfrac{1}{8}=\dfrac{2}{24}=\dfrac{1}{12}$

6. $\dfrac{7}{8}\times\dfrac{7}{8}=\dfrac{49}{64}$

14. $\dfrac{1}{5}\times\dfrac{1}{5}=\dfrac{1}{25}$

8. $\dfrac{1}{6}\times\dfrac{1}{3}=\dfrac{1}{18}$

Division of fractions

2. $\dfrac{4}{7} \div \dfrac{4}{7} = \dfrac{4}{7} \times \dfrac{7}{4} = \dfrac{28}{28} = 1$

4. $\dfrac{5}{6} \div \dfrac{1}{6} = \dfrac{5}{6} \times \dfrac{6}{1} = \dfrac{30}{6} = 5$

6. $\dfrac{9}{10} \div \dfrac{1}{10} = \dfrac{9}{10} \times \dfrac{10}{1} = \dfrac{90}{10} = 9$

8. $\dfrac{1}{6} \div \dfrac{1}{4} = \dfrac{1}{6} \times \dfrac{4}{1} = \dfrac{4}{6} = \dfrac{2}{3}$

10. $\dfrac{4}{5} \div \dfrac{4}{5} = \dfrac{4}{5} \times \dfrac{5}{4} = \dfrac{20}{20} = 1$

12. $\dfrac{5}{6} \div \dfrac{1}{6} = \dfrac{5}{6} \times \dfrac{6}{1} = \dfrac{30}{6} = 5$

14. $\dfrac{6}{7} \div \dfrac{5}{8} = \dfrac{6}{7} \times \dfrac{8}{5} = \dfrac{48}{35} = 1\dfrac{13}{35}$

Mixed-number review: Convert the following mixed numbers to improper fractions

2. $5\dfrac{1}{2} = \dfrac{11}{2}$

4. $2\dfrac{3}{4} = \dfrac{11}{4}$

6. $2\dfrac{2}{3} = \dfrac{8}{3}$

8. $4\dfrac{1}{2} = \dfrac{9}{2}$

10. $3\dfrac{1}{3} = \dfrac{10}{3}$

12. $4\dfrac{5}{6} = \dfrac{29}{6}$

14. $1\dfrac{1}{3} = \dfrac{4}{3}$

Decimal review: Addition with decimals

2. $\begin{array}{r} 4.50 \\ +\ 6.33 \\ \hline 10.83 \end{array}$

4. $\begin{array}{r} 5.25 \\ +\ 6.00 \\ \hline 11.25 \end{array}$

6. $\begin{array}{r} 4.89 \\ +\ 1.30 \\ \hline 6.19 \end{array}$

8. $\begin{array}{r} 8.65 \\ +\ 6.25 \\ \hline 14.90 \end{array}$

10. $\begin{array}{r} 4.44 \\ +\ 6.66 \\ \hline 11.10 \end{array}$

12. $\begin{array}{r} 8.00 \\ +\ 6.00 \\ \hline 14.00 \end{array}$

14. $\begin{array}{r} 12.45 \\ +\ 14.85 \\ \hline 27.30 \end{array}$

Subtraction with decimals

2.
$$\begin{array}{r} 9.99 \\ -\ 8.88 \\ \hline 1.11 \end{array}$$

4.
$$\begin{array}{r} 50.00 \\ -\ 33.33 \\ \hline 16.67 \end{array}$$

6.
$$\begin{array}{r} 36.25 \\ -\ 14.89 \\ \hline 21.36 \end{array}$$

8.
$$\begin{array}{r} 14.00 \\ -\ 12.95 \\ \hline 1.05 \end{array}$$

10.
$$\begin{array}{r} 16.90 \\ -\ 5.95 \\ \hline 10.95 \end{array}$$

12.
$$\begin{array}{r} 12.25 \\ -\ 11.50 \\ \hline .75 \end{array}$$

14.
$$\begin{array}{r} 35.86 \\ -\ 14.84 \\ \hline 21.02 \end{array}$$

Multiplication with decimals

2.
$$\begin{array}{r} 12.65 \\ \times\ 2.00 \\ \hline 25.3000 \end{array}$$

4.
$$\begin{array}{r} 4.44 \\ \times\ 2.22 \\ \hline 9.8568 \end{array}$$

6.
$$\begin{array}{r} 420.00 \\ \times\ 10.00 \\ \hline 4{,}200.0000 \end{array}$$

8.
$$\begin{array}{r} .87 \\ \times\ 1.00 \\ \hline .8700 \end{array}$$

10.
$$\begin{array}{r} 1.25 \\ \times\ .2 \\ \hline .250 \end{array}$$

Division with decimals

2. $2.89 \div .80 = 3.6125$

4. $2.59 \div .62 = 4.1774$

6. $\dfrac{3.35}{.35} = 9.5714$

8. $\dfrac{8.99}{.60} = 14.9833$

10. $2.99/.50 = 5.9800$

12. $2.50/.89 = 2.8090$

14. $1.25\overline{)6.99}\;\; 5.5920$

16. $.40\overline{)3.95}\;\; 9.8750$

CHAPTER 5

Round the following numbers.

2. 7.6 = 8

4. 44.50 = 45

6. 22.45 = 22

8. 254.443 = 254

10. 2,204.33 = 2.204

12. 10,000.6 = 10,001

Estimate the following quantities.

2. 30% of the 90 reservations will order the special: 27 guests will order the special

4. 20% of the 90 reservations will order prime rib: 18 guests will order prime rib

Ratios:

2. The vegetable salad has a ratio of 4 parts tomato, 3 parts asparagus, 2 parts avocado, and 1 part cucumber. The total quantity needed is 20 pounds.

STEP 1. **Add the number of parts: 4 + 3 + 2 + 1 = 10. The total number of parts is 10.**

STEP 2. **The total quantity needed is 20 pounds.**

STEP 3. **Divide the total quantity of product by the total number of parts: 20 ÷ 10 = 2.**

STEP 4. **Multiply each part by the quotient in Step 3. 4 × 2 = 8 pounds tomatoes, 3 × 2 = 6 pounds asparagus, 2 × 2 = 4 pounds avocado, 1 × 2 = 2 pounds cucumbers.**

Proportions:

2. The recipe for pie crust uses 12 ounces of flour to 4 ounces of butter. If you have 24 ounces of butter, how much flour do you need?

STEP 1. **Set up ratio.**

$$\frac{4}{12} = \frac{24}{x}$$

STEP 2. **Isolate x.**

$4x = 12 \times 24, 4x = 288, x = 288 ÷ 4$

STEP 3. **Solve for x.**

$x = 72$ oz. flour = 4.5 pounds

CHAPTER 6

Recipe	New Yield	Old Yield	Multiplier
B	200	100	200 ÷ 100 = 2
D	50	100	50 ÷ 100 = .5
F	150	25	150 ÷ 25 = 6
H	45	20	45 ÷ 20 = 2.25
J	15	60	15 ÷ 60 = .25

CHAPTER 7

2. 4 quarts = 1 gallon

4. 2 pints = 1 quart

6. 3 teaspoons = 1 tablespoon

8. A *fluid ounce* is a volume unit of measure. Volume is used for liquids.

A *weight ounce* is a solid unit of measure. It is used for nonliquid units of measure.

There are some liquid items that are measured using a weight unit of measure. The product used in a deep fat fryer is one example.

10. 454 grams = 1 pound

12. A multiplier can be used to convert between U.S. units of measure and metric units of measure because the relationship between the units is constant; it does not change.

14. A recipe calls for 1.5 kilograms of meat. You purchase 5 pounds of meat at $2.25 per pound.

a. The multiplier for kilograms to pounds is 2.2046.

b. 1.5 kilograms = x pounds. 1.5 × 2.2046 = 3.3069 pounds

c. You have enough meat for this recipe.

d. 5 pounds − 3.3069 pounds = 1.6931 pounds

e. The total cost for the meat used in the recipe is: 3.3069 × $2.25 = $7.44

16. Convert the following from U.S. to metric units of measure.

Ingredient	U.S. Units	Metric Units
Chicken stock	.5 gallon = 2 quarts	2 qts. × .946 = 1.892 liters
Chicken	1 pound	1 lb. × .4536 = .4536 kg
Carrots	.25 pound	.25 × .4536 = .1134 kg or .25 × 453.5924 = 113.3981 g
Potatoes	.75 pound	.75 × .4536 = .3402 kg or .75 × 453.5924 = 340.1942 g

CHAPTER 8

2. Define the term "edible portion."

The edible portion is the amount of usable product available after preparation and cooking. The edible portion is served to the guest.

4. Fill in the Yield Percent column:

$$\text{Yield percent} = \frac{\text{EP weight}}{\text{AP weight}}$$

Item Number	As Purchased	Edible Portion	Yield Percent
2	5 pounds	2 pounds	$^2/_5$ = .40 or 40%
4	1 kilogram	500 grams	$^{500}/_{1000}$ = .50 or 50%
6	1 quart	8 fl. oz.	$^8/_{32}$ = .25 or 25%
8	4 liters	1 liter	$^1/_4$ = .25 or 25%
10	40 pounds	15 pounds	$^{15}/_{40}$ = .375 or 37.5%

Fill in the AP Quantity column:

$$\text{AP quantity} = \frac{\text{EP/AS quantity}}{\text{Yield percent}}$$

Item Number	EP/AS quantity	Yield Percent	AP Quantity
12	1 gallon	30%	$^{1}/_{.30}$ = 3.33 gallons
14	11 pounds	65%	$^{11}/_{.65}$ = 16.9231 pounds
16	2 kilograms	75%	$^{2}/_{.75}$ = 2.6667 kilograms
18	64 fl. oz.	10%	$^{64}/_{.10}$ = 640 fl. oz. = 5 gallons
20	15 pounds	15%	$^{15}/_{.15}$ = 100 pounds

Fill in the EP/AS price:

$$\text{EP/AS Price} = \frac{\text{AP price}}{\text{Yield percent}}$$

Item Number	AP Price	Yield Percent	EP/AS Price
22	$3.25	70%	$^{3.25}/_{.70}$ = $4.6429
24	$5.00	50%	$^{5.00}/_{.50}$ = $10.00
26	$ .50	33%	$^{.50}/_{.33}$ = $1.5152
28	$1.00	10%	$^{1.00}/_{.10}$ = $10.00
30	$2.50	75%	$^{2.50}/_{.75}$ = $3.3333

CHAPTER 9

2. What factors or conditions create a yield variance between AP weight and EP weight?

Give specific examples.

Cleaning: Vegetables lose weight when dirt is washed off; lettuce.

Trimming: Vegetables lose weight when trimmed for presentation; broccoli.

Cooking: Meats lose weight when roasting.

Portion size: The amount of product available is too small for a full portion.

4. Which food product groups have a 100% yield?

Dairy, canned tomatoes, eggs, frozen produce, fat and oil, and flour and sugar.

6. What does the term *fabrication* mean?

To make an item recipe ready or ready to be cooked.

Yield Test Review Problem:
AP rib primal
AP weight 35 pounds
AP price per pound $2.09   Total price = $73.15

a. What is the total AP cost for the rib primal?

After Fabrication	(×)	Market Value	(=)	Total Value
20-pound oven-ready rib roast		$3.99 per pound		$79.80
4 pounds stew beef		$1.99 per pound		$ 7.96
5 pounds short ribs		$1.59 per pound		$ 7.95
3 pounds beef bones		$0.55 per pound		$ 1.65
3 pounds beef fat		$0.07 per pound		$ 0.21

b. Fill in the total market value per item column.

c. What is the total market value for the entire rib primal? (total of rib roast and by-products)

$97.57

d. What is the yield percent for the rib roast from the rib primal?

20/35 = 57.14%

e. What is the total yield for all of the by-products?

35/35 = 100%

f. What is the cost of the oven-ready rib roast fabricated from the rib primal? (Remember to sub-tract the market value of the by-products.)

$73.15 − ($7.96 + $7.95 + $1.65 + $0.21) = $55.38

g. What is the market value of a 20-pound oven-ready rib roast?

$79.80

h. Which product should be purchased, the rib primal or the oven-ready roast? Why?

The rib primal should be purchased if the employees can butcher the primal into an oven-ready roast and the stew beef and beef ribs can be used.

If the employees cannot butcher the rib primal and the by-products cannot be used, the oven-ready roast should be purchased.

CHAPTER 10

2. What information from a standardized recipe is used to calculate a recipe's cost?

Ingredient quantities, AP units of measure, yield percent, EP unit of measure.

4. What information is required to calculate a portion cost?

EP/AS portion size and every other item served to the guest.

Complete the following standardized recipe cost forms to determine the total recipe cost and the cost per portion.

STANDARDIZED RECIPE COST FORM

Baked Crusted Tuna

Recipe Yield: 26 pounds
Portion Size: 8 ounces
Number of Portions: 52

Total Cost: $254.4010
Cost per Portion: $4.8923
Date:

Item	Item Quantity	AP Unit of Measure	AP Cost per Unit	÷	Average Yield Percent (or Other Unit of Measure Info)	=	EP Cost per Unit	×	Item Quantity	=	Recipe Item Cost
Tuna, dressed	26 EP pounds	Pounds	5.99	÷	65% or .65	=	5.99/.65 = 9.2154	×	26 × 9.2154 = 239.60	=	$239.60
Olive oil	1 C	Liter	2.39	÷	1 C = 237 mL	=	2.39/ 1,000 = .0024 per mL	×	237 mL × .0024 = .5688	=	$000.5688
Fresh lemon juice	1 qt.	Pound	.79	÷	(2 C = 1 pound)	=	2 C = .79	×	4 C = .79 × 2	=	$1.58
Bread crumbs	1 gallon	Pound	.59	÷	(2 qts. = 1 pound)	=	2 qts. = 1 pound = .59	×	4 qts. = 2 pounds = 2 × .59	=	$1.18
Fish stock	.5 gallon	Quart	1.29	÷	100%	=	.5 gal. = 2 qts.	×	1.29 × 2	=	$2.58
Parsley	5 ounces	Pound	12.50	÷	100%	=	12.50/ 16 oz. = .7813 per oz.	×	5 oz. × .7813	=	$3.9065
									Recipe cost:	=	$249.4153

Recipe Cost Plus 2% for Misc. Items	**Total recipe cost:** = × 1.02 = $254.4036

Tuna: The EP cost per pound for tuna is $9.2154.

Olive oil: Purchased by the liter, used by the cup. There are several ways to calculate the cost per cup. Above I calculated the cost per mL and the number of mL in a cup.

There are 33.8 fl. oz. in a liter and 8 fl. oz. in a cup. 2.39/ 33.8 = .0707 per ounce × 8 = .5657. You can also use the multiplier to change liters to quarts.

CHAPTER 11

2. Food cost percent pricing: Fill in the blanks.

Formula I: Food Cost ÷ Food Cost Percent = Menu Price

Food Cost	÷	Food Cost Percent	=	Menu Price
$2.50	÷	30%	=	$8.3333
$4.18	÷	35%	=	$11.9429
$8.11	÷	10%	=	$81.10
$9.29	÷	25%	=	$37.16
$12.79	÷	45%	=	$28.4222

Formula II: Menu Price × Food Cost Percent = Food Cost

Menu Price	×	Food Cost Percent	=	Food Cost
$6.95	×	10%	=	$0.695
$15.95	×	30%	=	$4.7850
$40.00	×	40%	=	$16.00
$80.00	×	20%	=	$16.00
$200.00	×	38%	=	$76.00

Formula III: Food Cost ÷ Menu Price × 100 = Food Cost Percent

Food Cost	÷	Menu Price	×	100	=	Food Cost Percent
$0.96	÷	$7.95	×	100	=	12.0755%
$3.12	÷	$15.95	×	100	=	19.5611%
$1.89	÷	$9.95	×	100	=	18.9950%
$2.67	÷	$7.95	×	100	=	33.5849%
$22.38	÷	$125.00	×	100	=	17.9040%

4. In your opinion, which pricing method is better to use: food cost percent or contribution margin pricing. Why?

This is an opinion question. Therefore, every answer is correct.

CHAPTER 12

2. What are the advantages of each of these pricing options?

a. The original à la carte menu:

Each item is priced individually; generally a higher average guest check is produced.

A predetermined food cost percentage is easy to maintain.

b. The original table d'hote menu:

The guest orders a full meal, so it is a better value for the guest.

c. The contribution margin à la carte menu:

This method produces the best chance for profit because profit is built into each item.

d. The contribution margin table d'hote menu, which is a prix fixe menu:

This menu offers value to the guest and profit to the restaurant.

4. Which of these four options do you feel Thomas should use in his restaurant, *Tomas*? Please explain.

Thomas would be best served with option 4 because a new operation has to impress the guest and make money.

6. Contribution margin menu pricing: Calculate the base menu price for the following scenarios.

Scenario A

Total operating expenses:	$16,500.00
Total capital expenses:	$8,900.00
Total costs	$25,400.00
Plus the profit	$10,000.00
Total costs and profit	$35,400.00

Total number of customers: 1,200.

Base menu price is: $35,400.00/1,200 = $29.50

Scenario B

Total operating expenses:	$21,300.00
Total capital expenses:	$13,000.00
Total costs	$34,300.00
Plus the profit	$15,500.00
Total costs and profit	$49,800.00

Total number of customers: 2,500.

Base menu price is: $49,800.00/2,500 = $19.92

Scenario C

Total operating expenses:	$14,250.00
Total capital expenses:	$7,000.00
Total costs	$21,250.00
Plus the profit	$8,000.00
Total costs and profit	$29,250.00

Total number of customers: 1,400.

Base menu price is: $29,250.00/1,400 = $20.8929

Scenario D

Total operating expenses:	$10,050.00
Total capital expenses:	$6,500.00
Total costs	$16,500.00
Plus the profit	$15,000.00
Total costs and profit	$31,500.00

Total number of customers: 800.

Base menu price is: $31,500.00/800 = $39.3750

CHAPTER 13

2. What is a staffing guide?

A staffing guide is a table that matches the number of employees scheduled to the number of guests to serve.

4. What is a forecast of customer counts?

It is an estimation of the number of guests that will visit per meal period.

6. What are the advantages of forecasting prior to preparing the weekly employee schedule?

The advantages are to ensure the level of customer service is adequate and the cost of labor is controlled.

8. What other components are included in the payroll calculations for employees?

Social Security taxes, local, state, and federal employer costs, income tax, and benefits.

Staffing Guide and Schedule:

10. Using the following information, create a staffing guide and a schedule for the dishwashers at a local university's student cafeteria.

The cafeteria is open from 6 A.M. to 10 A.M. for breakfast, seven days a week. Five hundred students are eligible to eat in the cafeteria, but the average number of students for breakfast is 250. The average customer counts are as follows:

6 to 7 A.M.	25 students
7 to 8 A.M.	75 students
8 to 9 A.M.	100 students
9 to 10 A.M.	50 students

The dishwashers wash both the pots and pans used for food prep and the serving dishes. The cafeteria needs 1 dishwasher per hour for every 25 students. The minimum shift is 2 hours.

Staffing Guide: Dishwashers

	Number of Students	Number of Dishwashers
6 to 7 A.M.	25 students	1
7 to 8 A.M.	75 students	3
8 to 9 A.M.	100 students	4
9 to 10 A.M.	50 students	2

Schedule: Dishwashers

	Sunday	Monday	Tuesday	Wednesday	Thursday	Friday	Saturday
6 to 7	1	1	1	1	1	1	1
7 to 8	2	2	2	2	2	2	2
8 to 9	1	1	1	1	1	1	1
9 to 10	2	2	2	2	2	2	2

CHAPTER 14

2. Why is it important to manage the quantity of products in inventory?

The products in inventory represent money in the bank vault. If too much quantity is in inventory, too much money is tied up. If too little quantity is in inventory, the chances of not being able to serve guests their desired item increase.

4. Why is the cost of food sold calculation so important for the restaurant operator?

The cost of food sold calculation is so important because it displays the actual cost of food for the month, which then represents the food cost percentage. It also tells the operator if they have the correct quantity of products in inventory.

Integrated cost of food sold and inventory turnover rate problem:

	October 20XX	November 20XX
Beginning inventory	$5,400.00	?
Purchases	$15,250.00	$18,500.00
Ending inventory	$4,800.00	$5,200.00

a. What is the dollar value of food available for sale in October?

$5,400.00 + $15,250.00 = $20,650.00

b. What is the cost of food sold in October?

$20,650.00 − $4,800.00 = $15,850.00

c. October's sales revenue is $50,000.00. What is the food cost percent for October?

$15,850.00/$50,000.00 = .3170, or 31.7%

d. What is the beginning inventory for November 20XX?

$4,800.00

e. What is the dollar value of food available for sale in November?

$4,800 + $18,500.00 = $23,300.00

f. What is the cost of food sold in November?

$23, 300.00 − $5,200.00 = $18,100.00

g. November's sales revenue is $60,000.00. What is the food cost percent for November?

$18,100.00/$60,000.00 = .3017, or 30.17%

h. What is the inventory turnover rate for October?

$5,400.00 + $4,800.00 = $10,200.00 / 2 = $5,100.00
$15,850.00/$5,100.00 = 3.1078

i. How many days did it take to turn over the inventory in October?

30/3.1078 = 9.6531 days

j. What is the inventory turnover rate for November?

$4,800.00 + $5,200.00 = $10,000.00/2 = $5,000.00
$23,300.00/$5,000.00 = 4.6600

k. How many days did it take to turn over the inventory in November?

30/4.6600 = 6.4378

CHAPTER 15

2. List the advantages to the foodservice operator of using inventory and purchasing software.

IP software keeps track of a very large dollar value of inventory. It tracks which restaurants have taken items and therefore the cost of the items, and it alerts the operator to the need to purchase items when inventory levels reach a certain point.

4. What type of control procedures should be used with paper guest checks to ensure that all food prepared in the kitchen is paid for by the guest?

The guest checks should be sequentially numbered, assigned to servers, and audited at the end of every meal period.

Index